"Ellie Kay's financial advice is as good as gold. Straight-forward, practical, no nonsense advice from America's most frugal mom. This is not a finger-wagging lecture, it is friend-to-friend, heartfelt advice. Every family can benefit from *A Mom's Guide to Family Finances*."

—Dave Meurer
Author, *Stark Raving Dad* and *Out on a Whim*

"She did it again! Just when I thought Ellie Kay could not write anything better, she produces the world's most practical book on family finances. This is a book with real answers for real people dealing with real finances in a real world!"

—Phil Waldrep
Phil Waldrep Ministries

Books by Ellie Kay

A Mom's
GUIDE
to Family
Finances

ELLIE KAY

© 2004 by Ellie Kay

Published by Fleming H. Revell
a division of Baker Publishing Group
P.O. Box 6287, Grand Rapids, MI 49516-6287
www.revellbooks.com

Spire edition published 2006
ISBN 10: 0-8007-8735-8
ISBN 978-0-8007-8735-6

Previously published in 2004 under the title *A Woman's
Guide to Family Finances* by Bethany House
Publishers

Printed in the United States of America

To Wendy Wendler,
a wonderful friend

❧ ACKNOWLEDGMENTS ❧

There are many people behind the scenes that help a book come to life. I want to thank Steve Laube, my former editor and current literary agent, for his excellence, expertise, and knowledge. Julie Smith and Julie Klassen, my editors at Bethany House, have been tireless in their extraordinary efforts to help this book take its present shape. Kudos to Teresa Fogarty, my publicist, who is fearless in her marketing efforts and so accommodating to my many requests. Hugs go to Carol and Gary Johnson and Steve Oates for treating me like a queen.

I also want to thank my family for being patient as I hit the keyboard—my love goes to our children: Daniel, Philip, Bethany, Jonathan, Joshua, Missy, and Mandy. And a special hug goes to my Beloved for doing double duty as I write, travel, and speak.

One final note to the family of many fine friends at Bethany House as you have gone through so many changes in this last year: God bless you abundantly for forty-plus years of giving the world books that change lives.

❧ CONTENTS ❧

⊰ INTRODUCTION ⊱

In *My Big Fat Greek Wedding*, Toula laments the fact that her old-fashioned father will not allow her to take college classes and work in her aunt's travel agency. Her mother assures her that she will bring him around to the idea. She says wisely, "The men may be the head of the house, but the women are the neck and they can turn the head any way they want." In this movie, Old World meets New, and in each, a woman's influence is as powerful as ever.

A woman can have tremendous influence in the area of her family's finances, too. I wrote this book to help women achieve a sense of empowerment, direction, and victory in their family's financial situation.

Sometimes managing money gets old. But in this book, I provide women with a fresh approach to an important topic with safeguards built in to help guarantee success.

I've heard from many women who have been able to get out of debt, slash their household expenses, and make their financial dreams a reality. For example, Kelli from New Mexico wrote:

> We are a family who have always had hard times financially. My husband barely makes enough

to keep us fed, and some weeks we panicked because we didn't have enough money for food. Then I read Ellie's book, and she showed me, step by step, how to cut my food bill and save money in other areas, too. Within the first two months, I cut my food bill in half and have a ton of extra food! Now I can afford health insurance for the first time in many years.

I also want to help women learn how to take charge of their money so there will be less stress in their marriages. With "money arguments" cited as the number one reason for divorce, I believe this book can help strengthen and safeguard relationships. A reader from Little Rock, Arkansas, wrote:

> Our group selected Ellie Kay's book as the "Book of the Month" for June. I was a little skeptical at first because I don't enjoy SAVING money as much as I like SPENDING it. This has been a source of conflict between my husband and me for YEARS. To my surprise, Ellie's book was so funny that I couldn't put it down. Her practical tips were as simple and "painless" as she claims them to be. This spender has turned into a saver and been better off because of it. (My husband says Ellie saved our marriage!)

Since you've picked up this book, my guess is that you really care about your family's finances and want to improve your situation. In that regard, this book is from one woman to another—from girl friend to girl friend. I have been where you are and sincerely want to help you. Because whether you are a stay-at-home mom, your family's sole breadwinner, or anywhere in between, you play a critical role in your family's financial success.

Where *Did All the* Dough *Go?*

one

Meet the Bensons

I'll admit it. We're not normal.

But I think "normal" is overrated anyway.

I mean, a normal family doesn't have seven kids.

A normal dad doesn't have a bumper sticker on his Ford Escort that says, "My other car is an F–117 Stealth Fighter Jet."

A normal mom doesn't have to replace two garage doors in a year because she keeps backing into them.

A normal mom doesn't appear on a Satellite Media Tour covering fifteen cities in the morning and then cook Hamburger Helper at night.

I think the only family that may be slightly more abnormal than the Kays are the Osbournes. But we won't go there.

My kids tell me that I'm the most "abby normal" mom that they know, evidenced by something I did last summer. Although it wasn't horror flick material, my husband, Bob, found it quite horrifying.

I had two basic goals that I wanted to accomplish by the time I was forty years old—and time was running out. They were: (1) have twins, and (2) go skydiving. Since Bob refused to help me with the former, I decided to take care of the latter myself.

The annual bookseller's convention was in Atlanta, Georgia, and I decided to take the plunge after the main events were over. When I told my husband, Mr. Fighter Pilot himself, his response was: "You can't do that! It's too dangerous!"

Hello?

He's the one who lost hydraulics in his F–117 jet and had to rely on a parachute to stop him on the runway last month—only one second away from a disaster! And he's telling *me* skydiving is too dangerous?

My girl friend Vicki couldn't be talked into jumping, but she reluctantly agreed to accompany me on the adventure and to call Bob if the chute didn't open.

People asked me if I was scared over the prospect of climbing up to the ten-thousand-foot altitude to freefall back to earth, and I said, "No, I'm not."

If the truth be told, there *was* one moment when I had the wee-wee scared outta me. It wasn't when my instructor began strapping me to him in the airplane, which indicated we were two minutes from jumping— that was a moment full of anticipation! It wasn't when we opened the door and jumped, doing somersaults in the air—that was invigorating! It wasn't even when we were freefalling and giving the thumbs-up sign to the other instructor who was making the video—that was too fun for words! And it wasn't when we finally pulled our chute and the jerking motion carried us back up into the air—that was death-defying!

No, the only time I got scared was when we were peacefully floating to the ground and I was admiring the view. I should have been suspicious when my instructor told me his name was Mr. Jack Hammer, but it truly *was* his name. He was about forty-five years old, had his hair in a single braid that went down to his waist, and was the veteran of about three thousand jumps. This instructor was pointing out the landmarks, showing me his mobile home, the target where we would land, and the road we traveled.

He spoke into my ear. "Do you like this adventure?"

Yes! This is amazing!

He replied, "Do you think you'd like to come back, and will you tell all your friends about us?"

I thought that he was just doing a good job of marketing the skydiving school as I answered, *Sure! I'll tell all my friends about this!*

"Do you think your friends would actually come skydiving?"

I don't know, but I'll sure tell them.

His next words made my blood run cold. "Are your friends as pretty as you are? Because you're *real* pretty!"

This guy was strapped to my back at five thousand feet, and he's telling me that he thinks I'm pretty? YIKES! My response stopped him dead in his tracks.

Yep, my husband, the Stealth Fighter Pilot, thinks I'm pretty, too! Did you know that his jet is so accurate it could drop a bomb in the corner of your mobile home?

Jack immediately "backed off" (so to speak), and I didn't have any more trouble out of him! I suppose Jack the Hammer was just acting like a "normal" guy. But if that's normal, I'm glad I'm not.

Now I'd like to introduce you to the "normal" American family, whom we'll call the "Bensons."

Here's the lowdown on the typical American family:

• They are married with children—two, to be exact.

- They live in a modest three-bedroom, two-bath home with a yard and a lazy cat.
- They don't have a household budget.
- They have an annual income of $43,000.
- They owe about $8,000 in credit card debt.
- They have two car payments.
- They have a thirty-year mortgage.
- Their savings account has less than $500 in it.
- They have no long-term retirement account.
- They love their kids and want them to go to college.
- They are wondering, "Where did all the dough go?"

But the really amazing thing about the Bensons is where they *think* they will be one day. The Bensons believe that one day they are going to earn more money through raises, a better job, or profit sharing. They hope they will receive an inheritance or stop paying child support. They figure that someday there will be no more tuition payments and that childcare costs will go away when the kids are in school—thus cutting down on their monthly expenses. Then they'll finally have some breathing room. They also believe:

- One day they will no longer have a mortgage payment.
- One day they'll have their credit cards paid off.
- One day they'll have a nice savings account.
- One day they'll get a couple of IRAs.
- One day they will be able to send their kids to college and still have a retirement for their golden years.

But they have no plan! They think it will "just work out." One day, that is. One fine day.

Hello?

The hard fact about the Bensons is that if they continue the way they are now, with no real plan, they will:

- Pay five times as much on their house as it is worth.
- Increase their credit card debt.
- Never get out of consumer debt.
- They will get a second mortgage on their home to pay for their kids' college expenses.
- They will never acquire enough savings to retire comfortably.
- They will always have car payments.
- They will never realize their financial goals.

The Bensons are not really living what we imagine to be the American dream, are they? Unfortunately, they represent the typical family.

But your family doesn't have to be the same way.

You may be typical, as well. You may see a lot of your own family in the Bensons' realities and in their dreams. But you don't have to share their destiny. You don't have to be normal—being normal is overrated, remember? You *can* be different. You *can* find financial freedom. But it won't just happen. You can begin to chart a different course by answering the following question: *What are you willing to do today in order to make your family's financial dreams come true in the future?*

I'm not talking about get-rich-quick schemes or money-making pyramids. I'm not talking "business opportunities" or Internet scams. The question is: What are you willing to do to help your family become above average in a below average world? This little book that you are holding in your hands contains the keys to financial freedom. No, you won't be a millionaire and retire at forty. But you can learn how to get out of debt. You may not learn the nuances of investing in a bull

market or how to maximize your real-estate investments—this isn't that kind of a book. But you *can* learn
how to be in a position to help your kids through college without borrowing on our future. You can teach
those kids by your example that you don't have to live
paycheck to paycheck. You can give them a brighter
financial future than what you had when you got married.

But you have to make the decision that your family
will not be like the Bensons.

Will you rise to the challenge?

I hope so.

What are you willing to do today in order to make your family's financial dreams come true in the future?

Families are in desperate need of a safeguard for
their financial future. There are some basics that *every*
family needs in a crisis as well as for future security. The
following won't solve every financial crisis or problem,
but it is a good start to securing your family's financial
future. Some of these are easy to take care of, while others will have to be worked through carefully with your
spouse and family as you read through this book. Here,
then, are five areas that comprise your family's basic
needs:

1. An Emergency Savings Account This account is
not an investment account; it doesn't include IRAs,
401(k)s, or CDs. Its purpose is not growth but safety.
These are funds that you can access in the event that

you or your spouse is laid off or you have an emergency home repair or unexpected medical bills. The best way to build this account is to establish a family budget (see chapter 4, "The $50,000 Money Pyramid") and have this money automatically transferred into an account every month until there is at least three months' worth of living expenses in it for a dual income or six months' worth if you are a single-income family.

2. Life Insurance This is one of the easy ones that you can do for your family. It is important for you to see to it that your husband has enough insurance if he is the primary income provider in the home. But you will also need adequate coverage on yourself. When it comes to the primary provider, you will need enough coverage so that the financial dependents could invest the payout and live modestly on the proceeds. So figure a sum that would allow them to live comfortably assuming a 10 to 12 percent annual rate of return. Be sure you figure in social security benefits for dependents and any life insurance you or your spouse may already have provided at work. The two main types of policies are "whole life" and "term," with term providing the most coverage at the least cost. You can research the best policy for your needs at *www.iquote.com* (1-800-972-1104) or *www.quotesmith.com*. Or try *www.selectquote.com* (1-800-394-9006) and *www.termquote.com* (1-800-444-8376). These insurance agencies will provide comparative quotes on term policies that will meet your needs, and they will provide a credit rating for each insurer. This is a free source of information—you should never have to pay to get a life insurance quote!

3. A Will Here's another easy one. Bob and I have had a will ever since we were married due to the nature of his high-risk profession (and now, my high-risk hobbies!). The main section of this critical document will assign a guardian for your children. When we were in our childbearing years, we would call the guardians for our children and announce: "Guess what? We're pregnant—again." These dear friends would always reply, "We are praying for your health and safety!" Seriously, what could be more important? You don't want the state making decisions for you, which is what would happen if you do not have a will. In many states, the surviving spouse gets only one-third to one-half of the assets that were in your sole name. Your kids get the rest, and if they are minors, a court administrator will handle their money until they become adults! A simple will costs only $200 to $500 and is free for military members at the base's Judge Advocate's office. Do-it-yourself software packages are also available, and many communities offer inexpensive "How to Write a Will" classes, taught by a qualified attorney. Also, make sure that the beneficiary designations on your 401(k) plan, your IRAs, life insurance, and bank accounts are up-to-date.

4. A Retirement Account The Bensons did not participate in these accounts that were offered at their places of employment. You would be surprised at how many people do not take advantage of these terrific tax-deferred accounts, which include 401(k) and 403(b) plans. Now is the time to start one of these or an IRA and Keogh (more on these in chapter 6, "Paper or Plastic?").

5. A Good Credit Rating If you have to let your utility bills go unpaid for a couple of weeks to pay your credit card and mortgage payments on time, then do it! Of course, that isn't optimum—but one affects your credit rating and the other doesn't. (For more information on what affects your credit rating, see chapter 7.) Healthy finances need a good credit rating. "As a result of taking a three-week honeymoon, I paid my credit cards a week late," says Loretta Nolan, a financial planner in Old Greenwich, Connecticut. "It went on my credit report, and I had to explain it the next time I applied for a mortgage" (*Parade Magazine,* June 10, 2001). For a copy of your credit report, call one of the three national credit bureaus: Experian (1-888-397-3742); Trans Union Corp (1-800-888-4213); or Equifax (1-800-685-1111). There's a nominal charge, depending upon where you live, but it is worth it. The "Debt Diet" chapter, later in this book, will help tremendously in this critical area.

6. A College Fund for Those Babies! Some families have just about finished paying for their kids' college expenses, when they suddenly find themselves helping to raise their grandchildren! Whether you're trying to help your children or your grandchildren through college, there are strategic ways to select an account with low fees and a good selection of investments, plus a tax break. One of the best buys today is a Qualified State Tuition Plan, which was approved by Congress in 1997. These are sometimes called 529 Plans, after the section of the Internal Revenue Code that permits them. The contributions to a plan like this will be tax-deferred and could even be tax-deductible from your state income tax if you are a resident of that state. When the money is withdrawn for college, it is only taxed at the student's income tax rate. Check on the plan for your state; the one in New York will let you start an account with as little as $25 and will allow several people to contribute to it (hint: parents *and* grandparents). Some of these plans are better than others, so be sure to find the one that is right for you. Up to $100,000 can be contributed per student (let's see . . . that's up to half a million dollars for the five Kay kids that are still at home). If the child does not go to college, the money can be designated for another beneficiary or removed at a 10 percent penalty.

7. An Internet Connection I thought I'd end with another easy one—one that you probably already have. As simple as it may sound, Internet access is one of the best financial moves you can make for your family because it allows you to research virtually any financial topic with a few clicks. In the chapter "Room by Room Savings," you'll find that this is a fabulous way to save on the essentials, and in "Movin' On Up" you'll see how easy it is to research mortgage rates and reduce your monthly expenses in that way. Of course, you'll want to safeguard your children with a family-friendly filter to limit what they have access to, but used wisely, the Internet is a fabulous tool.

Play Money Versus Real Money

Self Test

When you were a kid, did you ever play Monopoly? He who gathered the most money, properties, and hotels won the game, right? I remember as a child that I pretended all the money I had was real. Winning with $10,000 in my pile was a great feeling!

Adults can play Monopoly with the game of life in a figurative sense by viewing real money as if it were play money—not considering the consequences of incautious spending habits. We tell our kids that "Money doesn't grow on ATMs!" But in many families, ATM withdrawals account for as much as 20 percent of the month's spending, and they cannot account for the majority of those dollars! Another dangerous game people play with money is debt. We charge vacations, Christmas gifts, and car repairs as a matter of course, knowing that there isn't any real money to cover the money we've borrowed to play the game of life.

One way to begin to move from play money mode into real money mode and view our finances with realistic glasses is to realize our money personality.

———

There was an old Cherokee chief who told his grandson about two wolves who were fighting. The first wolf was named anger, envy, sorrow, regret, greed, arrogance, self-pity, guilt, resentment, inferiority, lies, false pride, superiority, and ego. The second wolf was named joy, peace, love, hope, serenity, humility, kindness, benevolence, empathy, generosity, truth, compassion, and faith. The grandson asked his grandfather, "Which wolf will win the fight?"

The wise old man replied, "The one you feed."

———

In regard to money, the evil wolf sometimes hides in Granny's clothing and wears a mask of false security. Oftentimes people put on the "good" mask, pretending that they hold healthy values regarding money and that their finances are in decent shape—but a closer look reveals that this is not the whole truth and probably is anything but the truth. This charade is the same as playing with play money as though it were real money— pretending you have money you don't have. It can be embarrassing to admit that you're behind on your bills, you don't have a savings account, or that you don't live on a budget. One family counselor said, "Most people would rather talk about their sex lives than the truth about their money."

The first step in unmasking the wolf and making your finances something Granny would be proud of is to conduct an assessment of where you tend to view money as play money—spending what you really don't have or using money to compensate for other emotions in life, such as sadness, anger, or feelings of inadequacy.

In the first chapter, I gave a list of the basics that should be in every family's financial files. In this chapter, we're going to evaluate where you are financially so that you can chart a healthier course.

In the self test below, you will find ten basic money questions. Give yourself a number ranking between one and ten for each question using the following scale:

Rarely or Never	Sometimes	Frequently or Yes
1 ———————	5 ———————	10

1. Do you currently live on a budget?
2. Do you consistently stick to your budget?
3. Do you buy something only because you really *need* it? (Not just because you want it.)
4. Do you give 10 percent of your income to your church or other nonprofit organization?
5. Do you regularly give away material possessions?
6. Do you have a total consumer debt load of less than 10 percent of your annual income? (For example, if you earn $50,000 a year, you have a (non-mortgage) debt load of $5,000 or less.)
7. Do you save at least 10 percent of your income?
8. Do you have a savings account with at least two months' worth of income in it?
9. Do you own a retirement account or mutual fund of any kind (including 401(k)s, Roth IRAs, etc.)?
10. Do you buy something because a commercial convinces you to buy it?

Everyone has a money personality that generally fits on one end of two categories: you are either a spender or a saver. After you tally your score, take a look at where you fit on the following chart:

30 or less You are in the greatest need category and have all the characteristics of a born spender who has never made any modifications in her financial habits. If you haven't filed for bankruptcy yet, it is possible you will do so within the next two years unless you change your course and set it for financial recovery. If you are in this category, I suggest you call your local Consumer Credit Counseling Agency and set up an appointment.

Between 30 and 50 You are below average in your savings tendencies. You likely have a large amount of credit card debt and are headed down the path of financial despondency unless you make some critical changes now.

Between 50 and 70 If you are like a typical American family, you are somewhat content with the status quo but believe your family's financial situation will somehow right itself on its own. You tend to have a lot of characteristics of born spenders, but there is still hope for your born saver characteristics to kick in and save the day (and the money!). You are a prime candidate to become financially healthy rather quickly if you will rise to the challenge and make the changes your family needs.

Between 70 and 85 At least one of the partners in this family is likely a born saver with an ability to influence the household budget and other financial aspects in the home. This person may know many of the right things to do financially but could still lack some of the accountability to follow through in specific areas. Perhaps there has been a specific event that has derailed your finances, and you're ready to get back on track. If you make just a few modifications in your family's financial plan, you will be in a position to eventually help others who have great financial difficulties.

Between 85 and 99 You have a great financial situation and outlook. However, you are in danger of becoming out of balance in your financial situation if it has become an obsession or compulsion to save and invest your money. If you are still giving away 10 percent of your income, this indicates that you are not completely out of balance. You need to be sure that you find flexibility and latitude in navigating your family's finances.

> *We so often hear that we are what we eat, but in even more essential ways, we are what we spend—and how we spend it. —Dr. Ruth Berry*

100, or a perfect 10 Besides the fact that *you* could be writing this book, you need to be aware of the characteristics described in the previous paragraph. If you can honestly say that you have balance and are still generous with your money, then you might want to consider mentoring others to help them in these critical areas. However, because you are perfect, you may be lacking understanding of those who are not. Finding ways to use your gifts and talents to help others can keep you humble and compassionate.

Money Personalities and Emotions

Money can be a very emotional issue, and taking the mini test in the previous section can elicit both positive and negative feelings. Dr. Ruth Berry, a certified financial planner and college professor, has extensively studied families and their emotional attachments to money. As a former member of the board of the Vanier Institute of the Family, in Canada, she discovered some interesting facts:

> People may be embarrassed if they have too little money and even more embarrassed if they have too much. People feel good about when they give money away and even better when they get something for nothing. . . . We so often hear that we are what we eat, but in even more essential ways, we are what we spend—and how we spend it. ("Talking About Money," December 2002, *www.vifamily.ca/tm/292/1.htm*)

When it comes to distinguishing the characteristics that separate born spenders from born savers and how these two can come together in financial planning, it's important to consider the emotions that emerge when an individual (or a family) tries to manage their finances. One problem is the tendency to focus on numbers (as in a budget or the cost of an item) rather than people. Consequently, our efforts to manage family finances are seen as a way of accumulating things rather than a way of enhancing relationships. It's easy to neglect the feelings that family members experience in their association with money. If we focus only on numbers and forget the individual needs in our family, we might not be able to find a financial management plan that is mutually satisfying. For example, we might end up producing a budget that looks good on paper but sets our family up for failure.

When family members place the person and their

needs ahead of the numbers, there is ample motivation to find a balance when weighing needs with finances. We'll explore some specific emotions, such as denial, depression, and anger, in chapter 3, but let's take a look at some of the common money personalities in the family tree. As you read these definitions, look for yourself, your partner, and other family members in the list. Keep two things in mind as you read:

(1) All people are made up of *several* of these personalities, but they tend to remain within the basic framework of a born spender or a born saver.

(2) Any personality can move *into* or *out of* balance at any time, which is both a source of hope and a word of caution.

Power Paul

Money can be the ultimate strategic pawn in the power game. "He who has the money makes the rules" is the basic philosophy of this personality. A woman (or man) who does not produce their own money independently may feel a loss of power with this person. If the primary breadwinner is a Power Paul, he will use this position as a means of control and to "keep his wife in her place." Conversely, a Power Paul can rarely handle a wife who makes more money than he does, because she is too much of a threat. This personality makes all the financial decisions, does not seek his partner's input, will not allow access to financial information, and uses all of these strategies as a means of securing a position of strength in the family. Please note that Paul is sometimes a Polly! Men may comprise the majority for this personality—but they don't own the market on it!

The primary means of bringing this personality into balance is to stress the value of non-financial contributions made by other family members. Dr. Berry observes, "Both partners will feel more powerful and secure in an egalitarian relationship in which they share the financial and non-financial burdens of the family, including the time demands of household work and child care."

Secure Samantha

Secure Samantha was raised in a family that was one step away from being homeless. She is motivated to save money by the powerful emotion of fear. She has memories of not knowing where the next meal was coming from and having to move from dingy apartment to dingy apartment in order to stay one step ahead of the bill collectors. Consequently, she has vowed, as Scarlett O'Hara once did, "I'll never go hungry again. As God is my witness, neither I nor any of my kin will ever go hungry again."

Not every Secure Samantha saves money because of a background of poverty; there are a variety of circumstances that birth this personality. But the common characteristic is the fear of not having enough for basic needs, retirement, the kids' college, a rainy day, etc. This personality may marry someone who represents financial security. They also tend to be born savers who want to add "just a little more" to their investment programs, as they never feel they have quite enough money in savings. The loss of financial security is about the worst thing that can happen to Secure Samantha. So when she says no to a family vacation, even when it has been budgeted—it is her insecurity speaking.

A possible solution to Sam's tendencies is to reconcile the internal "voice" that compels her to save with her family's short-term needs. Sam needs to realize that God is in control and her financial destiny is not entirely in her own hands. When this occurs, she will be in a position to trust a solid budget with reasonable savings and can overcome the need to secure her future by compulsively accumulating money.

Tightwad Tilly

Born savers have many overlapping traits and may even seem to be identical at first glance. However, there are shades of gray that paint them to be decidedly different. Tightwad Tilly is much like her sister, Secure Samantha, but Tilly doesn't save money based on a fear for security. She does it because she's cheap. Max Bazerman, a business professor and financial adviser, says that someone like Tilly, or a basic tightwad, "has an *emotional dread* of spending any money for anything and views the accumulation of money as an end in itself" ("Emotions and Money," December 2002, *www.familyhaven.com*). In this case, the "emotional dread" is not fear, it is an emotion that tends to be rooted in selfishness.

There is a difference between being "frugal" and being "tight." The former can still be generous as needs arise (see "Balanced Betty"), but the latter leaves below-average tips and tries to sell their surplus goods at a garage sale or on eBay *first* rather than give them away to a family in clear need. Obviously there is nothing wrong with selling our goods, but Tightwad Tilly's first thought when her daughter outgrows a Laura Ashley dress is "How much can I get for this on eBay?"

Tightwad Tilly is always looking for an extra buck and is more tempted to compromise her generosity in order to earn that buck. In contrast, Secure Samantha would think: *I can't give this dress away! I might need the money I can get from it to buy another dress for my daughter. If I gave it away, I'm afraid I might not have enough.*

But Balanced Betty (whom you'll meet in a moment) would first think: *Is there a family who has a little girl who could benefit from this dress? If not, I'll just sell it on eBay.*

Tightwad Tilly needs to be brought into balance because she is more likely to be tempted to compromise her standards for a quick buck. I knew one such tightwad, a man who took his family to church every Sunday and tithed regularly. And yet I watched him capitalize on a woman's impulse-buying tendencies at one of his garage sales. She paid $15 for a phone, and when she left, he laughed and boasted to me: "I work with her and have been helping her with her finances. She's a terrible impulse buyer and really shouldn't have bought the phone, but heck!" He laughed again. "I only paid $5 for it, and she was willing to buy it for $15! So I had to sell it to her."

We could even call Tightwad Tilly "Shifty Sheila," because there exists a selfish drive to save a dollar anywhere and everywhere—even at the expense of others or their own integrity. Am I saying that all tightwads are dishonest? Of course not! They are simply more likely to be tempted because of self-centered tendencies. Note that tightwads might give to nonprofit organizations but still refuse to be generous in other situations. An extreme version of this personality is also stingy with their time, talents, food, material goods, money, and even candy!

One Tightwad Tilly worked at a beauty salon that I frequented. When I brought my children, they would each get a small piece of hard candy from the candy jar, and one of my sons asked once if he could get a second piece to take home to his brother. I'll never forget Tilly's response to this six-year-old boy's request: "No, you are only allowed one piece of candy. You can't have any more!"

Furthermore, she was clearly irritated that the child had the nerve to make the request! I never went back to that salon. All I could think was, *If she's so tight with candy to a little boy, then what else is she holding back on? What might she scrimp on when it comes to giving me my money's worth for her services?*

As with *any* of these personalities, Tightwad Tilly can be brought into balance with concerted effort and a plan of action. If you see yourself in some of these descriptions, being aware of your tight tendencies can help you overcome them. As a start, concentrate on ways you can give that are fairly painless.

Worrywart Wanda

The interesting thing about Worrywart Wanda is that she can be either a saver or a spender—she's one of the few personalities that can swing either way. This personality is obsessed with money—she talks about it, thinks about it, and makes every decision based on it. She can have too little and worry about how she is going to pay the bills, send her kids to college, and fund her retirement. She is obsessed with the thought of money. She worries for pleasure, it seems. Or, at the other extreme, she can have plenty and worry about a variety of issues such as:

- Do people like me only because of my money?
- Why do people always hit me up for money?
- What do I say to all these family members and friends who ask me for a loan?
- What if I make a bad investment?
- What if I lose my money?

This personality can be brought into balance by beginning to shift her focus off of herself and on to God's provision. A good exercise for Worrywart Wanda would be to challenge herself *not* to use the word *money* for one day each week. And if she finds herself reverting back to that obsession, to discipline herself to think about other things.

Spendthrift Steve

Spendthrift Steve never lets his money see the inside of his pocket. Professor Bazerman describes this personality: "The spendthrift is greatly distressed by the possession of any money and wants to spend it all as soon as possible ... most people have elements of both the 'tightwad' and the 'spendthrift.' " A spendthrift is the born spender who is truly bothered by having extra money. This personality will oftentimes spend the annual bonus, the inheritance, the birthday money—well before he ever receives it! Debt is a major by-product of the spendthrift's makeup, and even if he is able to manage his debt load, he doesn't manage to set aside much for a rainy day.

Accountability is a major solution to Spendthrift Steve's money problems. He needs to find a financial counselor or trusted friend who is wise with money and who will make him accountable to set a budget and stick with it. This would be someone from outside of his marital relationship who can view the situation from an impartial standpoint and help him get the assistance he needs to follow through with financial goals.

Feel-Good Francine

Feel-Good Francine hits the mall whenever she feels sad, lonely, angry, or even when she feels good and wants to "celebrate." In the military, I have known more than a few "Feel-Gooders" who add a new piece of furniture, a different outfit, or remodel the bathroom when their spouse is deployed. Impulse buying is a common characteristic of someone who buys consumer goods based on emotions. The compulsive shopper who obsessively buys more and more to overcome a negative emotion is almost always a Feel-Good Francine.

The key to overcoming this personality's overspending habits is to find other alternatives as an emotional outlet (besides overeating!). This person needs to ask herself: "What else makes me feel better when I'm down—besides spending money?" If exercise or having lunch with a friend or listening to music in a hot bath makes her feel better, then she should make a list of these activities and check them off each time she's tempted to buy her way out of an emotional black hole. Feel-Good Francine can break free of this destructive cycle once she faces the decision "Give me liberty or give me debt" and chooses the former.

Love Ya Louie

Uncle Louie may look a lot like his wife, Aunt Feel-Good, because they are both very materialistic. However, Francine uses money to feel good about herself, while Uncle Louie uses money to make others feel good about him. Essentially, his money is a substitute for love and time. Both are hung up on things, but for different reasons. Louie never knows if people love him for who he is or just because he's buying. But in some ways it doesn't matter because he so closely associates love as expressed in the things he buys for others.

Power Paul is Louie's dad. The son's behavior is an outgrowth of his father's power and control. His dad controlled him with the use of money so that money became a representation of positive feedback. Louie doesn't use money to control people in the same way his dad did—yet he does use money to try to control people's opinions of him. In other words, he uses money to get people to like him and have a positive emotional response to him. Some people may confuse love with power, but they are two distinct approaches with similar results. For example:

Love Ya Louie's kids will grow up with no knowledge of the value of money. They will be far more likely to misuse their possessions because Dad will always buy them a replacement. Love Ya Louie is the big spender, and if he doesn't have the money to buy love, he'll borrow it. He has workaholic tendencies but is a nice guy in many ways. He's just confused about the purpose of money and the value of other things in life. Things like time with family, training his children, and being loved for who he is—not what he can buy.

Balanced Betty

She's so perfect it makes you feel sick—or convicted! Balanced Betty has just the right combination of all of these personality profiles. She understands what is truly important in life, and she tries to be generous with her resources while still maintaining an aggressive savings style. Betty realizes that her kids won't simply catch good habits, she has to teach them well. So she administers an allowance while encouraging her children to save, share, and spend wisely. She also helps them learn a hearty work ethic through earning their own money for larger items and being responsible for chores. Betty is in balance right now—but she wasn't always. She used to have debt problems and even fell prey to some compulsive expenses that nearly ruined the family's budget. She also realizes that there are no guarantees that the future will be trouble-free—she doesn't have ultimate control. So she's thankful in her diligence and keeps trying to hold her family's finances in balance in the process.

Having financial peace and hope rule your home is better than having your children remember a house full of greed and regret.

Keep in mind that all the money personalities I described, with the exception of Balanced Betty, were extremes. They contained elements of the first wolf from our opening story in some form. The final personality is the balance we want to achieve, and it is a personality that uses money for good purposes. It's fairly obvious that having financial peace and hope rule your home is better than having your children remember a house full of greed and regret. But just because you are naturally a certain personality does not mean you have to remain in that modality.

The point to these personality profiles is that people tend to move in and out of them on a regular basis—but within their basic tendencies as a born spender or saver. And *any* of them can move into the "Balanced Betty" mode at any time as easily as any other personality. For example, a born spender is on one side of the spectrum and a born saver is on the other side. Balanced Betty is in the center, and both extremes can be as close to balanced as the other. Born savers tend to believe that their personality is "right" or "best." But if you look at the undiluted versions of the extreme born savers, you will see that they are not balanced. So no matter what your predominant money personality, you can move toward balance at any time—all you have to do is choose to do so. You may be experiencing money angst as a result of your scores on the test, but the best solution to angst is action. The next chapter gives five points of action you can take toward financial recovery.

three

Five Stages of Financial Recovery

I've always been an exercise advocate. It increases my energy, keeps unwanted pounds at bay (when I'm not scarfing down Krispy Kreme doughnuts), and even improves my disposition. It's easier to exercise at some times than at others. I remember feeling extreme frustration while trying to get in my daily walk when we were expecting our youngest child, Joshua. I had Daniel (age seven) on a bike, Philip (age five) and Bethany (age three) in a double stroller, and Jonathan (age one) in a backpack. Of course, the baby whale was out front (he weighed 10 lbs. 6 oz. when he was born). It was tough to push that stroller and balance Jonathan on a tired back with my expanding middle leading the way.

I used to walk three miles, three times a week, right up until the last few weeks of pregnancy. But the thing that bothered me the most was not the physical exertion—no, it was the way people gave me "the look." I was in complete denial about what a comical sight I was and the fact that most people had never seen such a

walking circus before. After rounding up Barnum and
Ellie's circus clowns, I'd head out the door to do my
routine, and people would drop jaws and stare. Oh sure,
some were more subtle than others. Some would just
give us a sidelong glance. Others would openly gape.
There was one neighbor, in particular, who I was convinced called her friends and asked them to come drink
coffee on her porch at precisely 9 A.M. every Monday,
Wednesday, and Friday. I think she might have even
sold tickets for a front-row seat.

Bob said that one time a friend of his was driving
by with his windows down and saw me glaring at a
motorcycle driver who had slowed down for a better
look. This "friend" told Bob he overheard me shout,
"What are you lookin' at?"

I don't remember it that way.

Bob said I must have had a memory lapse due to my
"delicate" condition. Believe me, at that time the only
thing delicate about this determined mama was my ego.
I had to face the rude awakening that I was the neighborhood entertainment.

Sometimes families face a rude awakening when
they have a financial counselor crunch their numbers or
if they use an online source to do the same (there are
excellent tools found at *www.cfcministry.org* or at
www.moneycentral.msn.com under My Money/My
Accounts.) Pamela York Klainer, Ed.D., the author of
How Much Is Enough? (Basic Books, 2001), says, "When
you get all your finances together, and you see it all in
front of you, it's very jarring." Klainer says the typical
client response is "Is that all there is?" and "Is it
enough?" She even likens it to other news: "It's like

going to the doctor and getting on the scale. Now you have the data."

So when we have to face the hard facts about our finances, it's not always an easy transition. In fact, depending upon the severity of your financial situation, many families go through five different stages that are similar to the stages of grief: shock, denial, depression, anger, and acceptance. Let's take an in-depth look at each stage.

> *How would you feel about finding out the bottom line of your family's finances in front of a national television audience?*

Shock

I recently worked with various families in a reality television series called *Simplify Your Life* on a brand-new network called The Fine Living Network. It's a great premise for a reality show: examine basic problems that families have and bring in experts to solve their problems. I was a financial expert that was sent to work with families on a couple of different episodes. One of the families experienced firsthand the "rude awakening" that I described above: a moment of truth where the bottom line of their finances was revealed. How would *you* feel about finding out the bottom line of your family's finances in front of a national television audience with a camera pointed in your face? You can imagine the look that registered on the husband's and wife's faces. You guessed it: shock.

Their mouths dropped open, and they stared in disbelief at the figures on the paper I held. I spoke to them in a calm, soothing voice and assured them that the figures were accurate.

Shock is defined as a violent, unexpected disturbance of mental or emotional balance (*Webster's II, New Riverside Dictionary*). Consequently, the shock you feel at this stage will be directly proportionate to the predetermined belief you held about your finances. It wouldn't be a *violent disturbance* if you already knew your net worth was 50K *in the red*, and you're only mildly shocked at how those numbers look on paper. It still doesn't make you feel good, but it's not a severe shock. On the other hand, another family would suffer a severe shock if they thought they were only a couple of years away from being debt free—but the numbers indicate that if they continue paying the minimum balance and acquire *no new debt* it will take them *fifteen years* to become debt free. That is a severe and violent disruption of their emotional balance and will take time to absorb. Obviously, the latter would most likely be a state of shock longer than the former.

But keep in mind that shock isn't always a negative emotion. You could be pleasantly shocked that you are farther down the financial road than you thought you were. And that would be a pleasant shock (we should all be so shocked). It reminds me of a scene from *Fiddler on the Roof* when Tevya was told that "riches are a curse," to which he responded, "May I be so cursed that I never recover!"

Another benefit found in the state of shock is that it is the first step toward financial recovery. It may be a harsh reality, but it's a place to start, and you have to start somewhere. The shock phase can last anywhere from hours to months—depending upon the reality of where you are compared to where you thought you were.

Denial

This is the most common stage in financial recovery. In fact, some people never move out of this stage and end up with perpetual financial woes. M. P. Dunleavey, a hilarious staff writer for MSN Money, had this to say:

> Here I was thinking I'd conquered most of my financial demons, when I got burned by the oldest and most insidious: Denial. The evil Dr. Denial is short, bald and, for a demon, very persuasive. His official title, for the record, is "King of Willful Ignorance and Subtle Acts of Self-Destruction."
>
> "But really," Denial said in a brief phone interview, "I just do whatever people ask me to do: cover-ups, muddled thinking, head-in-the-sand jobs, that sort of thing."

Americans spend with one hand and use the other to cover their eyes.
—M. P. Dunleavey

Well, that may be a funny way to look at denial, but the truth of the matter is that the enemy does not want us to be financially free and will use all kinds of tactics to keep us in financial bondage. But once we face denial we can overcome it and be well on the road to recovery. Dunleavey goes on to say, "Recent surveys of consumer spending indicate that Americans spend with one hand and use the other to cover their eyes" (*www.moneycentral.msn.com,* December 2002). This statement is backed up by the following facts:

- Two-thirds of Americans aren't saving enough for retirement.
- The average credit-card-carrying household is sitting on a total balance of more than $8,500.
- According to a 2000 Consumer Expenditure Survey, U.S. consumers spend about $8 million a minute.
- Last year Americans dropped about $63 billion on various forms of gambling.

This last fact may seem a bit out of place when we are talking about financial recovery—but it's right on target! The more people deny the seriousness of their financial situation, the more likely they are to try to find a quick fix to the problem. In fact, denial makes us more at risk for the temptation to gamble, figuratively or literally. People in denial are easy prey for various get-rich-quick schemes that are rampant on the Internet and in your e-mail inbox.

According to Margo Geller, MSW, a wealth counselor at GV Financial in Atlanta, there are four red flags of financial denial. She says you are in trouble if:

- You find yourself in the same financial pitfalls over and over and you're not sure why. You are always paying late fees, missing payments, balancing bills, or perpetually short of cash.
- You find yourself behaving in ways you know you shouldn't, such as buying another suit on your credit card, eating out when you promised yourself you'd

cook at home, buying a special toy for your child for no reason.

- You are financially stuck and cannot get unstuck (you are unable to reduce your debt, or if you do, you are soon back into debt again).
- You find yourself using the following stupid rationales to explain the above:

    "I'll deal with it."

    "Other people do this all the time."

    "Right now this is more important."

    "I need to."

    "I don't care, I'll figure it out later."

(*www.moneycentral.msn.com,* December 2002)

Depression

My husband knew what had happened when he came home early from work and followed the trail of chocolate candy wrappers down the hall, up the stairs, and into our bedroom, where I sat curled up in my robe and fuzzy bunny slippers reading a book and drinking coffee.

"Did it happen again?" he asked compassionately.

"Yes," I replied, trying to stifle a sob.

"How much?" he asked in a soothing voice as I sat crying softly.

I took a bite of amaretto truffle. "Twenty dol-larrrrrrrrs!" I wailed.

Poor Bob; this happens every time I purchase something and then find out I paid too much. It's enough to drive a Savings Queen to drink (coffee).

Okay, so I'm exaggerating a wee bit. I have to confess that sometimes I look for the tiniest excuse to play hooky from life and stay in my robe a bit longer, make another pot of java, and snitch a good piece of Godiva.

Even though I make light of my need to bag the best bargain, a series of financial disadvantages *can* add up to a ton of problems. And when these problems come crashing down around us, it can be downright depressing!

This depression stage is characterized by any of the following:

- **Concentration:** An inability to concentrate on anything that has to do with finances. An avoidance of any type of discussion on the issue.
- **Insomnia:** You cannot sleep well because you are bothered by the apparent hopelessness of your situation and are preoccupied with worry over the steps that you must take for financial recovery. Another issue that robs you of your sleep is concern that your spouse or other family members will not be supportive in the recovery process.
- **Guilt:** There can be a great sense that you are responsible for where you are—whether that feeling is valid or not. Sometimes people take on the responsibility of their spouse's or their own circumstance (lost job, medical bills, and other catastrophic events), even when they are not responsible, and the result is feelings of guilt.
- **Dejection:** A predominant sense of disheartenment in which your spirits are down to such a degree that they contribute to a sense of depression.

Once again, the amount of time you spend in this stage will be directly related to the severity of your financial condition. Hopefully, you will pass quickly in and out of this natural step in the process of financial recovery. But if you find yourself unable to move from this state, I would suggest you secure the services of a qualified financial counselor. Go to the Yellow Pages and look up Consumer Credit Counseling Services. Be sure you call the nonprofit organization and not a for-profit look-alike. This service will give you a plan to emerge from your present state and will help you take the steps necessary to move to the next step. They can get credit card interest rates lowered, payments deferred, and help you with a decisive plan to emerge from the debt cycle.

Anger

It is sometimes said that depression is simply anger turned inward. The anger stage is sometimes scary because anger can be manifested through a wide range of emotions at a high-intensity level. It can be as mild as severe displeasure or as severe as outright hostility. When the number one issue cited in divorce today is "finances," you can see people in this stage of financial recovery end up in the "debtor's prison" of divorce court. Following are the top twenty statements people express in this stage of financial recovery. Some are justified and others shift the blame. I threw in a couple of responses that are clearly uncommon, but they're funny in an otherwise unfunny list—see if you can figure out which ones they are.

Top Twenty Reasons I'm Angry About Our Finances

- My spouse bought that new _____(fill in the blank), and that is why we're in financial trouble.

- My parents have tons of money; they could help us but they won't.
- Our _____(fill in the blank with neighbors, parents, siblings, friends, etc.) never have financial difficulties; they don't know what it's like to have problems.
- My spouse is a spender, and I have no hope of financial recovery as long as I'm married to him.
- My plan was to move to Bora Bora, but my spouse won't let me!
- My spouse got laid off of his job and we can't even pay our bills. I'm so angry at _____(fill in the blank with your choice of blame targets: from the company to the economy to the president or God).
- We had a family member hospitalized with a severe medical problem, and now we can't pay our bills. Why would God allow this?
- We work hard for our money and end up paying all that money in taxes—it isn't fair!
- The cost of living is so high where we live, we'll never get ahead!
- My spouse made a bad investment, and my children and I have to pay the price of his mismanagement!
- My ex-spouse has lots of money, and I have to work night and day to make ends meet; he doesn't deserve it!
- I always seem to be a day late and a dollar short, no matter how hard I try.
- I couldn't afford to go to college, and I'm stuck in a dead-end job.
- I got a college education, and I'm overqualified and underpaid for this job.
- I have a third-grade education and don't understand

why I'm not a corporate CEO yet.
- We've tried budgets, and they don't work for us because we can't stick to them.
- We've tried reading financial books, and they don't work for us.
- We've talked to a financial counselor, but it didn't work for us.
- We've got a reason why everything you've written in this book doesn't work for us.
- We're not to blame.

You will notice that there tends to be a lot of blame shifting in this stage.

Is it the best response to the circumstances?

No.

Is it typical?

Yes.

Is there a healthy alternative?

Yes.

The solution for this stage is to talk to someone, almost anyone, because talking through your feelings of anger will help defuse those feelings. It's obviously important that we not behave in a verbal or hostile manner toward family members. It's not going to help if you call your spouse a "fat, selfish toad" and pack your bags for Bora Bora. If you or your spouse have these tendencies, then it's important to have a mutually agreed upon third party present when you express these feelings—preferably a financial counselor or family therapist.

Pamela York Klainer, Ed.D., the author of *How Much Is Enough,* gives four suggestions for those who are reluctant to face the ugly truth in this stage.

- **Blame** Don't blame your spouse. Or your parents.

Or your lousy childhood. Or yourself. Stop playing the blame game, as it only generates more anxiety and escalates feelings of failure and incompetence.

- **Own Up** The flip side of not blaming yourself is to own up to your own mistakes and admit the places where you've fallen short financially. For example, the time you took a vacation instead of paying off debt.

- **Practice, Practice, Practice** Unless you are a genius at handling money, you are going to need to build your skills. Learn to budget, save, and invest. It takes time. Even the Williams sisters have to get on the tennis court on a regular basis to stay at the top of their game. "Cut yourself some slack," advises Klainer.

- **Mastery** We are all unique, and what works well for one family's finances will not work for another's. Some families love computer programs that organize their money. Others prefer self-help books. Or financial counselors. Or seminars. Become a master of your own methods of balancing your budget. Once you develop a level of confidence, it will help to eliminate fear, anxiety, and especially anger.

One final note on anger: Don't be afraid of it. Anger can be good. Anger can be your friend. It is the last step before acceptance and complete financial recovery. So if you see this characteristic in yourself or your spouse, and you deal with it in a proactive way, then anger becomes a good thing. A very good thing.

Acceptance

By the time you've reached this stage, you've dealt with all the icky issues: the *shock* over the bottom line of your financial situation, the *denial* that you've got a problem, the subsequent *depression* that occurs when you face the truth, and the *anger* you feel as you look around for someone to blame. By now you are ready to enter the last and final stage of complete acceptance.

This is not a stage where a fairy appears, your finances magically get better, and we read, "They lived happily ever after" as the credits roll. You know you've reached this stage when at least some of these elements are evident in your life:

- **Change** You've asked yourself what you need to change, and you're willing to make those changes now.
- **Responsibility** You've accepted responsibility for what you did to contribute to your current financial status and identified the possible reasons that have contributed to that choice (money personalities, inadequate budgeting allocations, giving in to keep-up-with-the-Joneses pressure, emotions, habits, etc.).
- **Accountability** It's not enough to accept responsibility. In order to make the changes stick, we need to talk it over with at least one other person in order to solidify our purpose and strategy. If you're married, this should be your spouse. In addition, you could also speak with a financial counselor or financially savvy (and trusted) friend who can keep confidences.
- **Hot spots** You've identified the hot spots of where you've fallen short financially so that you know what needs to be fixed.
- **Patience** If money has made you anxious in the past, you've now realized that there's hope. You real-

ize that with patience, you will eventually succeed. You are also more tolerant of you or your spouse making mistakes and learning from them. You are ready to keep going.

- **Escape** You realize that in order to achieve your previous goal of escaping to Bora Bora, you'd have to fly to Tahiti, take several boat trips, and swat mosquitoes the size of sparrows. You decide to cancel those reservations and take the family to Niagara Falls instead.

Put It Into Action: From Fighting to Freedom in Four Relatively Easy Steps

Now that we've looked at your money personality, the emotions associated with money, and the five stages of financial recovery, it's a good time to put what we've learned into practice. Studies indicate that you retain 10 percent of what you hear, 20 percent of what you read, and an amazing 60 percent of what you hear, read, and *do*. That's why it's so important to put these principles into action, and the best place to start is in the marriage relationship.

You retain 10 percent of what you hear, 20 percent of what you read, and an amazing 60 percent of what you hear, read, and do.

Most couples, when asked if they argue about money, will reply, "Well, we really don't *fight* about money, we just have some occasional *disagreements.*"

Yeah, right.

When Bob and I were newly married, he went into an electronics store to buy batteries and came out with a new VCR. We were $40K in debt and barely had enough money to buy groceries. But did we *fight* about his irresponsible, compulsive, selfish, horrid, despicable, and not to mention stupid decision to drop $300 on a new VCR when we didn't even own a TV? Nah. We just had a disagreement.

Okay, I'll admit it, Bob and I have more than *disagreed* about finances—we have gone to our respective corners and come out fighting! Especially in the early years of our marriage, when Mr. Born Spender and Ms. Born Saver tried to mesh together two vastly different views of money management.

According to Barbara Steinmetz, a financial planner in Burlingame, California, tension mounts between partners partly due to poor communication. "It usually happens because the two people involved aren't on the same page. One person thinks they have a shared goal of saving for a house, car, or retirement, and the other doesn't." I would also add that they may not agree on tithing or paying down consumer debt.

What can you do to get on the same sheet of music and head toward financial harmony? Sometimes one of the biggest keys to solving a problem is recognizing what triggers financial disputes. Once you know what the sources of strife are, you can steer clear of those trouble spots. Here are several factors that often contribute to financial discord:

- **Problem: A Spender Bender** This is an age-old

problem that began when Eve was willing to pay the price for that piece of fruit and convinced her husband to ante up, also. If one spouse is a born saver, then get ready for the sparks to fly when the born spender goes on a buying binge.

- **Solution: The Balanced Budget** The best way to begin to curb a spender's buying habits is to sit down and work out a family budget (see chapter 4). If you've "been there, done that" and it still isn't working, then do it again—in front of a family counselor who is familiar with principles of household budgeting.

- **Problem: The Done Deal** "This is when one person opens the credit card bill and—surprise!—sees the tab for the drum set, the new suit, or the night your mate took the entire office out for lunch," says M. P. Dunleavey, columnist with *www. moneycentral.msn.com*. "The fantasy here is that because it's a *fait accompli* your better half will let it go. Oh, but they don't!"

- **Solution: The Return Deal** With the average American family in $8,000 of credit card debt, we find that this "done deal" policy only leads to more debt—and family problems. If you still have the receipt and can take the item back for a refund, this is the quickest fix to the problem. Additionally, make it a family policy to always consult your spouse for purchases over _____(fill in the blank). Sometimes just the *idea* of calling to ask what your spouse thinks about buying that $500 suit is enough to help you forgo the impulse buy.

- **Problem: Where's the Money, Honey?** This is where you (or your honey) hits the ATM machine on Friday, and by Monday you have no idea where that money went. You have nothing to show for it. Nada. Zilch. Nothing.

- **Solution: Target Practice** The old saying "If you aim at nothing, you'll hit it every time" is particularly true in your family's finances. The solution lies in tracking the money. Keep a list in your purse or car of when you got that $200 from the ATM and where it went. This takes seconds to document and makes you think twice about spending carelessly.

- **Problem: Too Many Chiefs, Not Enough Indians** In New Mexico, we lived near several tribal villages, and there was always a tribal chieftan. Many financial problems stem from family members trying to grab control of available resources. If you're not careful, the kids can grab a large part of the control with all their needs and especially their *wants*.

- **Solution: Checks and Balances** In most families, one partner is better with money than the other. It's natural to put that person in charge of paying the bills and administering the household budget. But it's also crucial that the other partner knows where the money goes and how it is spent. I'm the better "money handler" in our family (big surprise), but we establish our budget together. Bob writes the checks, and I review the checkbook, so that we have built-in accountability.

"How good and pleasant it is when brothers live together in unity."   —Psalm 133:1

Money
Management
for Everyone

four

The $50,000 Money Pyramid

Budgeting

When I was a girl, I used to love summertime for a variety of reasons, such as swimming laps in our pool, babysitting for extra cash, and getting to go to summer camp. But most of all, I loved watching my favorite TV game shows. I used to daydream about being a contestant on *The $50,000 Pyramid* (which later became *The $100,000 Pyramid*) and *The Price Is Right*. I imagined how my friends would react when I told them I'd won the big money.

On the pyramid show, the contestant had to answer a series of questions that hinted toward the answer but did not use any of the same words found in the answer. In the final speed round, the contestant almost always had to get the answer on the first clue or there wouldn't be enough time to answer all the questions and win the big cash. I can visualize the set now with the golden triangles turning around exposing the question. My heart would pound as the clock audibly ticked down the seconds. When I knew the answer, I'd leap for joy, pretending I was winning my way up that triangle to the grand prize. Each pleasant sounding *ding* meant one step closer to big bucks, while each annoying *buzz* meant a wrong answer. Whenever I watched, I was the queen of scream at home—the show's greatest fan.

Years later, when Bob and the military moved our family to California, *The $50,000 Pyramid* was but a cherished memory in the heart of this queen of scream turned into queen of savings. However, *The Price Is Right* was still going strong. Several friends of mine would take the base's MWR (Morale, Welfare, and Recreation) bus down to Burbank from Victorville and try to get on that show. My game show cohorts told me that the show's producers screened everyone in the studio audience to see who would make the best contestants. Audience members didn't know who was selected until they called your name and said, "Come on down! You're the next contestant on *The Price Is Right!*"

I couldn't wait to live out my childhood fantasy and sign up for the monthly game show trip with MWR. My friends said the producer asked only one question: "What do you do for a living?"

They said the producer could tell who would do well in front of the camera based on how they answered the question. For example, if you were enthusiastic and outgoing, you were more likely to be selected. The night before we were to leave on the bus, all I could think of was "the gimmick." I just *had* to come up with something quick and snappy. My whole game show career was hinging on that one moment of fame—that one opportunity to impress a Hollywood producer. I played one scenario in my mind after another as the hours ticked by. Finally, at 3 A.M., it came to me like the right answer on the final question of *The $50,000 Pyramid*! I had my gimmick—and a prop. Now all I needed was a chance.

The next day we drove three hours to the studios and waited several more hours to be interviewed by the producer. We were in line, and it was almost my turn. When the big moment came, little did I know that I was about to discover a hidden talent within me that I never knew existed—the ability to catch a producer's eye.

"What do you do for a living?" the deadpan producer routinely asked.

Taking out a long grocery receipt I had tucked into my purse, I answered, "Well, this is what I do." I waved the receipt like a cheerleader's pompon. "I show people how to save 50 to 85 percent on their food budgets by using coupons to make sure that—" I paused for dramatic effect, then smiled—"to make sure that—the price is right!"

Well, apparently it's true that guys can't resist a cheerleader—he was hooked. "That looks like a price list, and we can't let a sweet little lady like you take a list of all the prices into our studio." He smiled, eyeing the receipt and testing my response.

I threw it at him. "Here, keep it!—" I smiled and winked—"As something to remember me by!"

Later in the studio, with the cameras rolling and Bob Barker holding his microphone, I heard the sweetest words on earth, "Come on down, Ellie Kay. You're the next contestant on *The Price Is Right!*" I can still remember the butterflies that were swarming in my tummy when I made my initial bid on the wicker desk.

Miraculously, I won the desk and then had the chance to go on stage to play, of all games—the grocery game! I won all the way up to $1,000, and when Bob

Barker asked me if I wanted to go for $10,000, I said, "I'll go for it, Bob."

Then, just as in my childhood memories, I heard the sound of an annoying buzzer indicating that my choice was wrong and I'd lost the $10,000! I wanted to cry. But I still had another chance in the "Big Spin" part of the show, where I tried to spin closest to $1.00 without going over.

I spun .95 on the big wheel and won the right to go to "The Showcase Showdown." This is where there are two contestants who vie for a showcase of prizes and merchandise. The one who comes closest to the actual price of the showcase, without going over, wins! Plus, if you bid within $100 of your showcase, you could win both showcases. It was one of the most exciting days of my life and a childhood dream come true.

When the models were showing the items in my showcase, I mentally added up the total and then added $2,000 more to the price because it always seemed that their prices were inflated. I'd practiced this a dozen times at home and now was my chance.

My showcase included a twenty-one-foot travel trailer, a video camera, vitamins, a *huge* silver punch bowl set with cups, and an eight-burner two-oven cooking range!

I bid $18,500.

The studio audience, who had been cheering for my spin, now turned fickle and booed at my bid. They thought I'd overbid. The other contestant made his bid and we went to a commercial break.

The lights were getting hot; I had broken out in a sweat, and my heart was beating so hard that I just knew the studio audience could hear it through my microphone. Finally Bob announced that we were back from the break.

Bob first went to the other contestant, who'd bid $14,000.

The demigod of daytime television announced, "Your actual showcase price was $13,990! Aw . . . you're $10 over! I'm so sorry."

Bob asked me how much I bid, and I feigned that I didn't remember, so he quipped, "You bid $33,000!"

The studio audience laughed at his joke, but all I could manage was a weak smile as by now both the audience and myself thought that my bid was probably too high. This would mean there would be no top winner for the day.

After what seemed like a lifetime, Bob Barker finally said, "You bid $18,500, and your showcase is valued at $19,600."

The queen of scream had won!

Because sometimes . . . childhood dreams *do* come true.

———

The amazing thing about that experience, my first time on national television, was that I was never nervous. I just concentrated on keeping my chin down while looking into the camera to get the best angle of my face (otherwise, I looked like I had a triple chin!). Ten years later I had my own television show called *The Savings Tip of the Week With Ellie Kay* in upstate New York. And now I'm on national and international television on a regular basis. This goes far beyond my childhood dreams!

Sometimes we dream about things that are more attainable than we can ever imagine. For example, you may be reading this book and dreaming (or scheming) of a budget you can stick to. You dream of having less debt—and seeing your financial dreams come true. It's more doable than you think!

There are six basic steps to keep in mind when creating a household budget:

1. Set goals. If you don't know where your family finances are going, how can you reach your desired destination? Goals are a road map to where you want to be.

2. Determine Current Spending. Write down everything you spend over a three-month period. If you spend cash, write down what it's for. This will help you discover how and where you are currently spending your money.

3. Determine Your Current Budget. Take the information from step 2 and put it into a budget chart (see next page) to determine what your current budget would look like based on your present spending habits. You will be able to recognize the excess right away and see where your problem areas are.

4. Create a New Budget. Now that you've seen where all the dough is going, it's time to redirect that dough into some bread that will feed your family for years to come. See the fresh approach to budgeting in the next section.

5. Measure Your Progress. Continue to keep records, and once a quarter assess your progress toward your financial goals. Are you paying down debt? Are you breaking the ATM habit? Are you building your savings accounts? During these sessions, you may need to reassess either your goals or your budget.

6. Reward Yourself! You can read more about this in chapter 10, "The Seventh-Day Rest." Your budgeting efforts should be a combination of hard work and fun, so create a reward system that accompanies each of the financial goals you have set for your family.

———

Part of the reason families have trouble sticking to a budget is that it seems way too complicated to create and even harder to keep! I've decided to try a fresh approach to establishing a household budget based on *The $50,000 Pyramid* model.

See what you think of this:

10%—FUN MONEY
30%—THREE KINDS OF SAVINGS
60%—ALL FIXED OR COMMITTED
EXPENSES

Hey! With "Fun Money" listed at the *top* of the pyramid, what is there not to like? But before you think we're back at chapter 2 and playing with "Play Money" again, let's look at some of the details of the Budget Pyramid to see just how doable it can be! As in the game, we'll start from the bottom level, or foundation first, and work our way up to the fun stuff!

The Foundation—Committed Expenses

Richard Jenkins, a financial columnist for *www.moneycentral.msn.com*, said, "What you're trying to do with a budget is to prevent overspending, which ultimately leads to piling up debt. Contrary to the

way most people budget, however, it rarely matters
what you're overspending on—dining out, entertainment, or clothes. Who cares? It's still debt, right?"
(*www.moneycentral.msn.com/articles/smartbuy/bsics/
8579.asp,* December 2002).

I'd never thought of it that way, but it makes perfect
sense. If you want to get down to the details of every
dollar on your budget, that's fine, too. But if you get a
good grip on your committed expenses, those that *have*
to be paid, and keep those to 60 percent of your budget,
then you'll be on the right track, too.

Jenkins went on to point out the following:

> Looking at my own spending history, I realized
> that it wasn't the little luxuries here and there that
> got me in trouble. It was the large, irregular
> expenses, like vacations, major repairs, and the hol-
> idays that did all the damage. To avoid overspend-
> ing, I had to do a better job of planning for those.
> And then there were the really big expenses: buying
> a car, putting a down payment on a new home, or
> putting a new roof on an old home—all of which
> can run into the tens of thousands of dollars. They
> also can often be postponed, sometimes for years,
> which theoretically should give me a chance to save
> for them.

*The key to managing your finances
well is to lower the numbers in the
"committed expenses" category.*

Just as when a builder is constructing a building he
must secure the foundation first, so we must secure the

foundation level of our finances in order to find success. If we change the foundation, we will also influence everything upon which that foundation is built.

The key to managing your finances well is to lower the numbers in the "committed expenses" category. Many of the expenses on this foundational level have been or will be discussed in later chapters—especially chapter 7, "Movin' On Up," which talks about mortgages.

Now is the time to go back and look at steps 2, 3, and 4 in the "Six Steps to Creating a Household Budget." Look at where you've been spending, what a budget would look like based on unchanged spending habits, and then come up with new numbers for your committed expenses as you create a new budget.

The basics in this category include the following but will vary depending upon your individual household and family's needs:

- Tithe
- Housing/Utilities/Taxes
- Clothing/Dry Cleaning
- Insurance (all types)
- Medical/Dental
- Transportation (loan, gas, and maintenance)
- Groceries
- Telephone
- Credit Card/Loan Payments
- All Other Non-Recreational Bills—even those that are nonessential (including cable services, dance lessons, violin rentals, etc.)

The Second Level—Three Kinds of Savings

On first review, you might think that 30 percent is way too much to put into a savings program, especially if you're currently living from paycheck to paycheck. But you need to take a closer look at what has been included in this level.

- **Long-Term Savings** These can be automatically deducted from your paycheck and placed into an interest-bearing money market, CD, or savings account that is fairly accessible. A portion of this money could also go into buying annual Roth IRAs or Education IRAs, such as a 529 plan. Violet Woodhouse, a certified financial planner (CFP), attorney, and certified family law specialist, in California, says she's constantly surprised by how many couples haven't bothered to set up a 529 plan to pay for their children's college education (Dunleavey, *www.moneycentral.com,* October 2002). Go to *www.savingforcollege.com* to request the program material from states that interest you.

- **Retirement Savings** This should also be automatically deducted from the paycheck and placed into a 401(k) contribution plan or another similar retirement plan.

- **Short-Term Savings** These can also be directly deposited from a paycheck into your credit union or bank savings account. These funds are ones that are easily transferred to your checking account. This fund could be placed in the "committed expenses" account because it is destined to pay for things such as vacations, household or car repairs, down payments, new appliances, holiday presents, and other expenses that will come up during the year. In other words, even though you are technically saving this money, it is short-term savings that are designed to pay ongoing expenses that will arise in your household. It's always great to have the savings to pay for those rainy days when the washing machine breathes its last, you find out your son needs braces, and your car needs a new transmission.

If you never see this 30 percent of your money, and your committed expenses have been budgeted without this additional money set aside, you will likely never miss it. Paying yourself first, in terms of savings, is an important aspect of planning for a rainy day and keeping the clouds out of your family's finances.

Fun Money

This money can be spent on anything you like so long as it doesn't exceed 10 percent of your budget. There are some suggestions later in this chapter to stretch those fun dollars even further. Here are some of the things included in this category:

- Dining Out
- Movies
- Day Trips
- Amusement Park Trips
- Manicures/Massages
- Concerts
- Hobbies
- Sports

Adjustments and Exceptions

At the risk of overstating the fact, please remember: Every family is different, and their financial needs will be different, as well. If you have a considerable amount of non-mortgage debt (30 percent of your committed expenses category), or if you have had an unusual circumstance that caused you to accrue debt (medical expenses, job loss, etc.), the $50,000 Pyramid model is a goal for you. Until you get your consumer debt paid down, I recommend you take 20 percent of your savings (for retirement and long-term savings) and pay down the debt. But don't even try to take this dramatic step until you've closed charge accounts at department stores and with credit card companies.

As soon as the debt is paid off, redirect that 20 percent back into the savings programs we've discussed. If you crunch the numbers and still can't get your expenses to fit on the foundational level of our pyramid, then chances are one of the following conditions exist:

- Your house owns you (see chapter 7).
- You have more car, RV, or boat than you can afford.
- Education costs for private school or college are more than you can afford.
- You are living beyond your means in "luxury" areas (beauty salons, massages, sculptured nails, housekeeper, dining out, impulse buying, CDs, DVDs, gadgets, electronics, clothing, etc.).

What can you do to reduce the committed expenses that exist in your budget in order to fulfill the obligations of the savings level? You are reading a book by a woman who wrote the book(s) on making ends meet. At one time our family had $40,000 worth of consumer debt and little to show for it! We learned how to save on everything and paid down that debt within two and one-half years. So it can be done. The rest of this chapter consists of ideas on how you can save money every day.

> *Wise shoppers can save hundreds of dollars each year in a minimal amount of time by simply doing their homework.*

Quick Cash—Ten Tips to Save Ten Bucks in Ten Minutes (or Less)!

In order to find some wiggle room in your budget, it's important to get a quick start by reducing in other areas. Many of the best ways to save require an investment of only ten minutes or less. Wise shoppers can save hundreds of dollars each year in a minimal amount of time by simply doing their homework. Here's how:

- **Price Matching** Many stores, including Wal-Mart, will meet or beat any store's prices. Look through the Sunday circulars before you make your regular trip to a store that matches competitors' prices (call the customer service department to see if they match other stores' sale prices.) Then *take the circulars* to the store with you and get the lower price. I saved $25 on groceries last week with this simple tool and $50 on a DVD player. I also saved time and gasoline by not having to travel to several stores to shop the sales!
- **Online Prices** For higher-priced items, go to the online site of your favorite store or check out their catalog. Get the best online price, print out the

price page, and take it to your local store to see if they will match it. Or, order online if they cannot match the catalog or online price. I ordered an office item from a mainline store's Web site this week. They had a special that had no shipping charge for orders of $50 or more. The company routed the delivery through my local store, and they delivered the product the next day (free of charge). I saved around $120 on the item.

- **Ask for Substitutions and Rain Checks** Many stores will substitute other items of equal or greater value on out-of-stock sale items. Several months ago a digital camera was originally priced at $139 and was on sale for $99. The retailer was out of the featured item and substituted an upgraded model—which was on the shelf for $189! At grocery, department, and drugstores, ask for a rain check if they are out of the sale item. The next time you shop, bring your rain check in and get the sale price.

- **Save at the Gas Pumps** Log on to *www. GasPriceWatch.com* to find the cheapest gas stations in your neighborhood. If you save just twenty cents a gallon, you'll have an extra $300 this year.

- **Home Insurance** You may be paying more for your home insurance than you need to because it's annually renewed and automatically charged to your escrow account. Request a copy of your homeowner's policy and shop around. It takes an agent only ten minutes to run a computerized quote that could save you several hundred dollars.

- **Service Shop Around** Besides insurance, there may be other services for which you are paying too much. Are you getting the lowest price for garbage pickup, online services, long distance, etc.? A few minutes of phone calls can save you big bucks. A friend of mine recently changed garbage companies and lowered her monthly bill from $45 to $20.

- **Selling Your Car** Go to *www.edmunds.com* or *www.kbb.com* to get an accurate value of your car before you sell it. Print out this sheet and show it to prospective buyers if necessary. Most people sell their cars for several hundred to several thousand dollars too little by not doing ten minutes' worth of research.

- **Check the Checker** As you are checking out *anywhere* be sure you are seeing what you are being charged. Over the course of a lifetime, the average person could be overcharged as much as 20 percent. If you are overcharged, bring it to the cashier's attention right away. Some stores even have an "It's right or it's free" policy, where if they charge you an incorrect amount, the item is free! I got a $16 double bag of diapers free when one of my local grocers, who had this guarantee policy, overcharged me.

- **Savings Links** At my Web site, *www.elliekay.com,* I have several money-saving links that take only minutes to access. Some of these values, such as major department store sales, can add up to as much as 50 percent with savings on fashions, travel, coupons, and free samples.

- **Entertainment*** Go to *www.entertainment.com* and enter your zip code to look over a regional coupon book. Before you buy, preview the book online to see whether it is worth the purchase price. If you frequent many of these local businesses already, it could add up to major savings. These include free oil changes, haircuts, restaurant discounts, movie theater passes, and more. The prices on these books range from $10 to $25, and the total savings amount depends on your area. For example, in Atlanta, Georgia, the book is $25 and has up to $6,500 in local savings. (*More on entertainment savings below under "The Honeymooners.")

- **Pizza! Pizza!** The next time you order pizza, ask them what the specials or coupon values are for the week. Three out of four pizza shops will give you the coupon value just for the asking—even if you don't have the coupons! You can save anywhere from 20 to 50 percent (on a buy one/get one free special).

The Honeymooners—Saving for Fun

I've reiterated how important it is to have money set aside for entertainment. It's only about 10 percent of your gross income, so that means you might have to be a bit more creative in your approach to entertainment, but it doesn't mean that you have to give up family fun, vacations, or date nights.

When I searched for my knight in shining armor, I never expected him to ride in on a jet. But alas, my knight was really a pilot nicknamed K-Bob, and his jet wasn't the only thing that flew at supersonic speed. *Time* also flew around this guy. When we were dating, we'd find ourselves lingering over pie and coffee at our favorite restaurant. We got so caught up in conversation that we were often shocked to discover we'd been talking for hours! My clue should have been when a new shift of waitresses appeared to refill our coffee cups.

When Bob proposed, I protested, "When I'm with you time flies so quickly that if I married you I'd be an old lady before I know it!" Eventually, I gave in and married the flyboy, just yesterday . . . or so it seems.

Many years later we have seven children and made twelve military moves, but our favorite "couple time" is still spent in a restaurant, chatting at dinner and lingering over coffee. But if you're not careful, a weekly date night can add up to big bucks and put a significant dent in your family's entertainment budget. You can learn to stretch a dollar just like great conversation over coffee and save significant date dollars to make those dinners *financially* palatable. Here are a few ideas:

- **FSIs** Free-standing inserts are the coupon inserts from your Sunday paper. Mainline restaurants offer great coupon values in FSIs that can add up to 50 percent off the bill, or almost $400 per year!

- **Newspapers** Quickly scan the "Living," "Variety," or "Entertainment" section of your local paper for weekly restaurant specials. It may require going out on a Tuesday instead of a Wednesday. What only takes about ten seconds to check can save you $10 (or more).

- **Internet** Find your favorite restaurant's Web site and check out their values. Many sites will offer printable coupons as well as weekly specials. Try looking under *www.[favorite restaurant's name].com*. For example, *www.bennigans.com*. On my Web site *(www.elliekay.com)* I have links to coupon sources such as *www.valpak.com* that find local coupon values based on your zip code, or *www.coolsavings.com,* where you are e-mailed info on great deals.

- **Two for One/One for Two!** If your fave place doesn't offer a "buy one/get one free" special, why not try the new trend of sharing a meal? This savvy approach is especially smart at a restaurant that's notorious for serving larger portions. You may have to pay a small surcharge for an extra plate, but your wallet (and waistlines) will thank you.

There is a lot of information in this chapter, but keep in mind that it wasn't designed for you to absorb all in one sitting. This is a chapter for you to dissect and work on one section at a time. So take a deep breath, exhale, and repeat. Remember that you don't have to do all of this in one day, one week, or even one month. Budgeting, saving money, and cutting back on household expenses is a process. The important thing is that you are making a start. If you go back and read this chapter once a month and try something new from it, you will be making progress. The worst thing you can do is to think you have to do it all at once and then get frustrated and quit. Life may not be a game show, but you *can* take the pyramid approach. First, lay a strong foundation (a budget), and then work toward your dreams one step at a time.

❧ five ❧
The Debt Diet

I delivered an eleven-pound baby. Do you know *how* a body that has been put through such trauma can try to regain some of the vim and vigor it had *before* birthing a baby whale? Well, the answer is simple, but it's not easy.

Diet and exercise.

Yuck.

Double yuck.

I've tried all kinds of fad diets, but it always comes back to diet and exercise if I want to shed those extra pounds. But we love the fads, don't we? I remember a girl friend, Cecille Alexander, in the sixth grade, trying an "ice cream" diet. That's all you could eat. Until you got sick of it. Twenty years later she still can't stand the sight of ice cream. Which is why I should probably develop a new diet called "The Chocolate Diet." All I could eat would be chocolate, tons of it, until I was sick of it. Then I'd never eat chocolate again and probably drop twenty pounds. Of course, there is a risk involved—I'm hoping I would get sick of chocolate before I gained twenty more pounds. On the other hand, if I gained five pounds in the eat-it-until-you-hate-it phase and then lost twenty pounds in the aftermath, that's a net loss of fifteen pounds! I think I'll start *now!*

But on second thought, what if I gained twenty pounds before I started hating chocolate, then lost only five (because the hate could not be sustained)? Then that would be a net gain of fifteen pounds, and I'd be a shoo-in for the keynote speaker at the Annual Whale Watchers Society convention.

Sigh.

There are no easy answers.

If you eat more than you exercise, you're going to gain weight.

You don't have to take my word for it, most experts agree: Diet *and* exercise are the only things that really work when it comes to weight loss.

Heavy sigh.

The only thing that really works is to spend less and save more.

Getting out of debt is like going on a diet—it may be simple, but it sure isn't easy.

The only thing that really works is to spend less and save more.

That's it. That's budgeting in a nutshell—the CliffsNotes version of the rest of this chapter. But don't stop reading! You may still learn a thing or two.

Oh sure, we have all these "new" and "improved" ways of looking at money. You can sign on with a for-profit financial counselor that promises the moon. You can try to win the lottery. Or fall prey to a get-rich-quick scheme. But if you spend more than you make, you're still going to be in debt. You could even understand all the reasons why you overspend and get in touch with your inner money self—but no matter how good you feel temporarily, you still have to come back to the cold, hard fact that you have to spend less than you make.

In his bestselling book *Debt-Free Living,* Larry Burkett said, "It is interesting that the increase in the American divorce rate can be tracked on a curve matching the growth of debt in this country." Debt doesn't benefit a marriage or a family, and it certainly doesn't benefit your future. Just as being overweight leads to health and emotional concerns, so debt has its consequences, as well. You may want to consider the following:

Reasons to avoid debt:

- Debt puts your marriage at risk.
- Debt makes you a servant to the lender.
- Debt borrows from your future.
- Debt hinders sharing with others.
- Debt erodes resources through high-interest payments.
- Debt promotes impulse buying.
- Debt makes you ugly.*
  (*This is Ellie's personal opinion and should not be attributed to Larry Burkett. ☺)

On the other hand, those who have a low debt load experience many benefits. They have the ability to give generously in order to meet the financial needs of others. There are fewer arguments over money in a household with low debt liability. You can answer your phone and not worry about having an answering machine to screen calls from creditors. The anxiety over floating the bills to make the minimum payments will not exist in a home that follows sound financial principles.

Stepping on the Scales—How to Know If You're Financially Overweight

You may not know if you really have a debt problem yet. You may have thought, *Hey, I've put on a few dollars here and there.* There's no more effective way to see if you have a problem than to step on the scale. Here are some indicators that you need to go on a debt diet.

- Using credit card cash advances to pay for living expenses
- Using and depending on overtime to meet the month's expenses
- Using credit to buy things that you used to pay for in cash (i.e., groceries, gasoline, clothing)
- Using the overdraft protection plan on your checking account to pay monthly bills
- Using savings to pay bills
- Using one credit card to pay another
- "Floating" the bills: delaying one bill in order to pay another overdue bill
- Using another loan or an extension on a loan to service your debt
- Using a co-signature on a note
- Paying only the minimum amount due on charge accounts

Gastric Bypass

If you are more than one hundred pounds overweight, your doctor may recommend an extreme surgery where food intake is restricted by interrupting the digestive process, sometimes through the removal of some of your intestines and/or a surgically restricted stomach size.

It's extreme.

It's expensive (around $15,000).

According to the Weight-Control Information Network, here are the benefits and risks:

Benefits

- Right after surgery, most patients lose weight quickly and continue to lose for eighteen to twenty-four months after the procedure.
- Although most patients regain 5 to 10 percent of the weight they lost, many maintain a long-term weight loss of about one hundred pounds.

Risks

- Ten to 20 percent of patients who have weight-loss surgery require follow-up operations to correct complications.
- Nearly 30 percent of patients who have weight-loss surgery develop nutritional deficiencies such as anemia, osteoporosis, and metabolic bone disease.

Financial Bypass Surgery

Can you guess the financial equivalent of this procedure? If your finances are in such a severe state that they require extreme measures, what would that be?

I'll give you a hint. It begins with a "b" and ends in a "why?"

Bankruptcy.

Why do people file for bankruptcy? Is it always due to financial mismanagement? No, it's not, and that is what clouds the issue for people who feel a moral responsibility to refrain from filing for bankruptcy. Here are the top five reasons cited for bankruptcy (not in any particular order):

1. Poor planning
2. Unemployment
3. Illness or injury
4. Divorce or separation
5. Business failure

Benefits

- Those who choose this option do have some debt eliminated while retaining some of their assets.
- You can generally still qualify for a mortgage, within very specific parameters.
- Gerry Detweiler, author of *The Ultimate Credit Handbook,* says, "Some people have no other choice; for them it is the best decision, and they will be able to rebuild their credit, get credit cards, and even a mortgage."

Risks

- It is extremely difficult to rise above the stigma of bankruptcy, as anyone who has ever filed will tell you. Feelings of guilt and inadequacy are the most common emotions experienced after filing.
- Bankruptcy puts a financial burden on our country. According to the American Bankruptcy Institute,

personal bankruptcy (non-business related) hit an all-time high of 1.5 million in 2001. Research by the Federal Reserve indicates: "Household debt is at a record high relative to disposable income. Some analysts are concerned that this unprecedented level might pose a risk to the financial health of American households." This should alarm all of us, as should their conclusion: "A high level of indebtedness among households could lead to increased household delinquencies and bankruptcies, which could threaten the health of lenders" (*www.abiworld.org,* December 2002).

- The rule of thumb that most experts recommend is that if a bankruptcy filing doesn't eliminate at least 50 percent of your debt, then the disadvantages will typically outweigh the advantages. You get tagged with a very bad credit report and run the risk of not getting out from under the debt that prompted the filing in the first place.

- Renting an apartment is the biggest issue for those who have filed for bankruptcy. Without the proper references, you are a high risk for landlords; they may refuse you based on your credit report. Or, they may require a higher deposit, plus the first and last months' rent.

- A bankruptcy filing stays on your record for at least eight years. You can't file again for bankruptcy for six years, and creditors know this and try to take advantage of the fact that you now have more disposable income.

Treating a Symptom, Not the Problem

Robin Leonard, who has written numerous books on bankruptcy, says that most people have little trouble getting credit after bankruptcy. "Many people describe coming home from work one day and seeing a letter from the bankruptcy court congratulating them on the discharge of their debts, as well as a credit card application" (*www.abiworld.org,* December 2002).

However, studies indicate that if you don't deal with the spending habits and financial mismanagement that likely got you into bankruptcy court, you will be back in debt within two years.

An Emotional Decision

Ultimately, this is an emotional decision based on a desperate and (seemingly) hopeless financial situation. I am often asked, "Should a Christian ever consider filing for bankruptcy?" Which is a question that sparks as much emotion and controversy in Christian circles as "Should a Christian ever get a divorce?" Even when Bob and I had $40,000 in credit card debt, we never considered filing for bankruptcy. Mary Rowland, an MSN financial columnist, wrote, "A recent poll of the top financial experts on bankruptcy took the hard line, advocating discipline and hard work to get out of debt" (*www.moneycentral.msn.com,* December 2002). I tend to concur with the rest of the Christian and non-religious financial experts: choose discipline and hard work to get out of debt. Here's a look at why most experts advise that you steer clear of bankruptcy.

Five Reasons for Not Filing

1. Personal Stigma In the movie *It's A Wonderful Life,* Jimmy Stewart, who plays George Bailey, has lost $8,000. In his lowest moment he cries out, "Do you know what this means? It means bankruptcy and scandal and even prison." While bankruptcy no longer carries some of those severe penalties, the stigma attached to this decision is a negative one that cannot be denied and must be considered.

2. Been There, Done That You can file for chapter 7 only once every six years; it cannot be repeated within that time frame—it's against the law.

3. Friends and Family Matters If you have asked someone to cosign for any of your loans, they will become liable for your debts. There are better gifts you could give your loved ones.

4. Filing Means You Defrauded a Creditor The fact of this filing is that you defrauded a creditor. The bankruptcy court will look carefully at recent expenditures. If there is evidence that you tried to hide assets, traveled extensively for pleasure, or lied about your income and debts, the bankruptcy judge will not be pleased.

5. Spending Spree If you recently spent a pile of money on luxury items, you might not want to file for bankruptcy. Last-minute luxury purchases are typically noted and disallowed in bankruptcy.

So You Want to Be a Lean Beauty Queen?

Extra pounds can creep up on you, and BOOM!— you're twenty pounds overweight before you know what hit your thighs. But there's usually a reason: you get out of the exercise habit. Possibly your metabolism slows down as you age, or you get into unhealthy eating patterns. Just as the beauty queen has looks, poise, and talent, some people start out with all the resources they need to succeed financially: talent, education, and a good job—but they end up getting into bad habits, and the debt fat creeps up on them. There are reasons why some people tuck money away with the regularity of a watchmaker, while others are head over heels in debt even with a six-figure income.

We've already explored some of these reasons in chapters 2 and 3, but let's take a very brief look at the profile of bankruptcy filers and see (1) what we can learn from their mistakes, and (2) what hope exists for those who have filed.

"Researchers like Professor Tahira K. Hira at Iowa State University, in Ames, argue that the traditional ways of helping people deal with spiraling debt, such as negotiating with their creditors and working out debt repayment schedules, will not help change the negative behavior pattern." Hira further states, "We need to sit down and understand why this person seems to have a consistent financial problem . . . or the same person will be in trouble again in five or six years" (Mary Rowland, *www.moneycentral.msn.com,* 2002).

There are three basic questions that should be asked of the person in serious financial trouble: (1) Who are you today? (2) What kind of experiences did you have growing up? and (3) How do you feel about yourself today?

The most consistent pattern, even with people of different socioeconomic backgrounds, is that they had weak family relationships as children and a below average social life in school. The self-esteem of those filing for bankruptcy was extremely low—which isn't a news flash, is it? The research also indicates that one or both parents were absent either physically or emotionally during a filer's childhood.

Sometimes it's easier to get a good feel for this group of people by looking at what they are not. For example, Hira says that the research group who had a "healthy attitude about money" generally had high self-esteem, were comfortable with money, and had the following characteristics in common:

- They had a pleasant growing-up experience.
- They came from an intact family.
- One parent had taken great interest in developing the child as a person.
- They were told, "You're beautiful, wonderful, capable, and you can do it."
- A parent had helped them open a bank account and manage it at a young age.
- They had role models.
- They had a value system.
- They had financial goals at a young age.

(Mary Rowland, *www.moneycentral.msn.com*, 2003.)

This kind of a background is why I wrote *Money Doesn't Grow on Trees: Teaching Your Kids the Value of a Buck* (Bethany House, 2002). We will look at practical ways to get out of debt in the next chapter and explore solutions to these financial problems in a pragmatic way, but it's important to consider the emotional and psychological elements that may be contributing to perpetual financial difficulties.

You may not have these problems, to this extent, but you may be the person to whom these people turn for help. The best help you can give is to encourage them to see a financial counselor. Chances are, if you cosign for a loan for a friend or relative, you will pay off that loan. If you bail them out of $7,000 worth of credit card debt today, they'll be back, asking you to do the same thing, in three years. They may even need psychological help to overcome some of the emotional associations with money that cause them to overspend. Sometimes the best help is to simply point them in the right direction.

Hope Floats (and So Do You)

Is there hope for those who already have a sizable amount of debt? Is there any use even *trying* to manage debt? The answer is a resounding YES. Getting out of debt may be easier than you think, even for major debt, such as a house. If you want a quick start to fixing this problem, you can try "The One-Hour Money Workout" below. Sometimes we quit before we start because the task seems far too great. If you have to lose fifty pounds, you concentrate on the first five pounds, not the entire amount! Set your timer and try this workout, which is a combination of a brainstorming session and a motivating exercise. The key is to keep the conversation and the activity moving along. You don't want to exhaust yourself with an eight-hour marathon session; this is just a quick start. Here's your first workout.

The One-Hour Money Workout

1. Make Up Your Mind Warm-Up (five minutes)

Bob and I have experienced the incredible miracle of overcoming seemingly insurmountable debt. As you know by now, when we got married, we had $40,000 in consumer debt. We were like many other young people who didn't realize the price we would pay for instant gratification.

We purposed to get out of debt and made immediate changes in our lifestyle to accomplish this. We also purposed to tithe 10 percent of all we made. We ended up living on less than 25 percent of one income in order to accomplish these goals. Within two and a half years we were debt free! We made up our minds, prayed to God for His help, and found the strength we needed to make that decision to become debt free. We haven't looked back since.

2. Couple Meeting Strength Training (ten minutes)

It usually takes more than one partner to get a couple into serious debt. Even if one person does most of the spending, the other spouse usually tolerates the destructive behavior in some way.

This meeting is a time to write down goals on paper so that you will have a tangible and objective standard to work toward. The goal you set should include: (a) how to stop spending more than you make, (b) how to pay the *interest* on the debt you have accumulated, and (c) how to retire the debt.

3. Budget Burn (twenty minutes)

Finalize and agree to your new budget. This may not seem like a lot of time on this topic, but you've already done some legwork earlier in this book. If you want to see another budget option, jump on the Internet and go to Crown Financial at *www.crown.org* or MSN Money.

4. Taking Your Heart Rate (twenty minutes)

This is the point where you get the facts on your credit and debt information so you can decide if you need to go to a professional financial counselor. Check your credit report and order a copy from any of the major credit bureaus: Equifax (1-800-685-1111), Experian (1-888-297-3742), or Trans Union (1-800-888-4213). This report costs about $8. If you live in Colorado, Georgia, Maryland, Massachusetts, New Jersey, or Vermont, or if you've been denied credit before, you qualify for a free copy annually. Or, you can get one online for the same fee at MSN Money.

In the meantime, I would recommend that you cut up all but one or two credit cards and cancel all other open credit accounts. This will help minimize the temptation to impulse buy as well as keep you on track with your goal of no new debt.

5. Congratulations Cool Down (five minutes)

Sit back and grab a glass of something cool to drink and reflect on all you've accomplished in just one hour! Keep in mind, you're building on what you've done so far, and you're in it for the long haul so you can have a checkbook that is at least as buff as your body.

You can't get out of debt by positive talking, only by positive doing.
—David Bach

The Guide to Healthy Living

Now that you've (1) realized you need to lose some debt, and (2) have gotten a quick start on dropping the excess debt, it's time to (3) dig deeper into the reasons why you have been overspending or living outside your means.

You've heard the saying "Garbage in, garbage out." The same applies to diet and finances. If your intake is good, you'll be healthier, but if you've been thinking thoughts like *I'll make more money later and pay it all off then* or *I can always cut back on expenses,* but you never do, then you're never going to get healthy. "You can't get out of debt by positive talking, only by positive doing," says David Bach, the bestselling author of *Smart Women Finish Rich.* The next chapter will give specifics on how to go about paying off your debt. In the meantime, you might want to grab a cold glass of ice tea and munch on a few carrot sticks—just to get in the mood!

❧ six ❧

Paper or Plastic?
Credit Cards

As I was running water over the Tupper-ware bowl, I kept thinking, *This is taking waaaaay too long. I'm going to miss out!"*

"Why were you in such a hurry?" you ask.

Why, I was getting my ice-logged credit card out of the Tupperware bowl so I could run back to the mall and buy a new microwave. It was on sale "today only, limited stock." But the real reason for my sense of immediacy was the admonition "*No* rain checks!" They had me there.

This was many years ago, and I had read in a finan-cial self-help book that if I had a problem with credit card spending, I should put the card in a bowl of water and freeze it. The idea was that it would be such a hassle to thaw it out, you'd have enough time to thoughtfully consider the purchase and avoid impulse buying.

Nice thought.

In theory, that is.

Take a moment and imagine a scenario with me: You're in the mall shopping with a girl friend. You've already had your Starbucks Decaf Venti Vanilla Latte (with soy milk) and gone by the Godiva store to check out their free samples. As you look in the window of your favorite mid-price-range clothing store, you see a gorgeous outfit in your color and size that would be perfect for you. The best part is it's on sale for 30 percent off! Normally, you might ask yourself: "Do I *really* want this?" or "Can I afford it?"

Instead, you ask yourself: "Is this worth thawing out my credit card for?"

Here's a word of advice. If you have to thaw that card, don't put it in the microwave, because it will (a) demagnetize the card, and (b) melt the card into a misshapen mess that once resembled a credit card.

Don't ask me how I know these things; I just did some . . . ah . . . research! Yes, that's it! I did research to discover these unusual facts in case you ever wanted to use plastic instead of paper money and you had all your credit cards on ice.

————

There are a lot of bizarre gimmicks out there to help you get out of debt. The best advice is to improve your financial health through plastic surgery—and cut up those cards. Seriously. My husband and I did it (well . . . um, that was *after* I froze them). It worked for us. In the meantime, we developed discipline through the ol' diet and exercise approach (spend less, save more) and we're in a completely different financial place than we were when we lugged around $40,000 in consumer debt.

The average consumer carries the largest percentage of their debt in credit cards—even more so than in a mortgage or car loan. That doesn't mean you can't cut the fat in these critical areas of housing and transportation (more about these later in the book). But the primary place that most families need to look is in their wallets at a thin little piece of plastic.

This entire chapter is dedicated to guiding you, as a personal trainer would, through the exercises involved in eliminating the debt fat that has accumulated through the use and abuse of credit cards.

Junk Food Junkies—Debt Consolidation

I admit it. I like an occasional bowl of potato chips, and I've been known to sneak a few of Joshua's french fries from his Happy Meal, but my hips don't appreciate the contribution. It's easy to get sucked into the fantasy of fast food and easy fixes. That's why the fantasy of debt consolidation can suck you into something that is bad for your financial health. Your e-mail inbox is probably flooded daily with promises from the debt consolidation industry that make claims such as "Debt relief is just a click away!" or "Cut your interest rate to 0 percent!"

Here are red flags that should go up when you consider consolidating those credit card bills:

- **Promises, Promises** If the company offering the loan offers to "take care of everything," red flags should go up in your mind. They make claims that they will negotiate lower interest rates and reduce your monthly payments in one easy step. But many of these debt consolidators build in a fee as part of the monthly payment you make to them! For example, you could be paying $60 for every $600 payment, which is the usual 10 percent fee they charge. Plus, these companies collect an additional 10 to 15 percent from the creditor when they pass along your payment. *It's not worth paying someone else to do what you can do yourself.* Go to the MSN Money Debt Consolidator at *www.moneycentral.msn.com/investor/ calcs/n=debt/main.asp* in order to find out how to consolidate your debts. For example, M. P. Dunleavey, staff writer for Money MSN, said, "The senior credit counselor at Integrated Credit Solutions [a debt consolidator] told me, in grave tones, that it would take me 379 months, or 32 years, to pay off my debt. With their services, however, they would 'save me 27 years,' and I could pay off my debt in just 53 months, or about 4 years." But when the writer went to the calculator listed above, it told her she could pay it off in 41 months, providing she was willing to make slightly higher minimum payments to each card: a total of just $60 extra per card (*www.moneycentral.msn.com*, 2002).

- **The Easy-Does-It Loan** This is a hard money loan that claims to be easy to get. But the truth of the matter is, if you need a loan, chances are you've already missed a few payments and your credit history is less than sterling. Some of these consolidators might entice you with the "ease" of obtaining the debt consolidation loan but could end up charging you *more* interest than you're paying now—even as much as 21 or 22 percent! You might end up with lower payments, but you'll pay over a longer period of time, resulting in more money out of your pocket.

- **Balance Transfer Trick** You've seen the low-interest cards that are a dime a dozen, but the rates last only a few months, and then you have to switch cards again in order to find another low interest rate. This

activity shows up on your credit report and is oftentimes negatively interpreted. If and when your activity finally catches up with you, and the latest low
interest card will not approve you, you are left paying the higher interest on the card you are holding
in your hand. If you've already done this, then for-
mally close down those accounts and ask the credit
card company to mark the account "closed at the
customer's request." Otherwise, it will appear that
the creditor closed your account—which would
make you look like a poor risk, even though you are
trying to get your credit paid off.

Confessions of a Happy Meal Addict—The *Right* Way to Consolidate Debts

There are times in our lives when we have that
watershed moment and realize that we have a problem
that needs to be rectified. Mine was when Joshua and
Jonathan asked their papa to take them to get their
Happy Meals instead of Mama, "because she always eats
our fries."

Sigh.

You see, I never buy fries for myself. They're
unhealthy. They're bad for me. Why . . . I don't even
want them, you see.

Well, not really.

I *want* them. But I shouldn't have them. So I don't
buy them. Instead, I do the "right" thing and buy a
salad for myself and then steal my children's food.

Likewise, you may recognize your need to consolidate your debts, but let me warn you that you will be

tempted to stray—even as you're doing the "right" thing. For example, as you consolidate and pay off cards, you will likely feel a relief in your monthly expenses and start "splurging" again in the fatty areas of your budget.

Before you consolidate or make another move toward credit card relief, decide right now that you will apply all extra monies to paying down this debt. Here are some unexpected sources of income that should be applied toward debt reduction:

- Inheritance
- Income tax refund
- Overtime
- Bonus
- Insurance dividend refund
- Pay raise
- Any other unexpected additional income

Now back to our regularly scheduled program that was interrupted by a trip to Mickey D's. We were talking about the right debt consolidation moves. Here are a few of the best options, but keep in mind, once again, that your family has unique needs and abilities. Some of these options may not work for your financial situation. Others may be a perfect fit that help you get financially fit:

- **Home Equity Loan** This is an obvious choice but one that should be used only with great restraint. Oftentimes, people will do something like the Bensons did: they took out an $8,000 home equity loan to pay off $5,000 worth of credit card debt and take a $3,000 vacation to Disneyland. Hello? That's no better than stealing your child's french fries. In fact, it's worse, because you're borrowing from your family's future and teaching your kids that if you want it now, then finagle a way to make it happen.

The primary advantage to a home equity loan is that it tends to carry low interest rates (currently in the high single digits), and the interest you pay is tax-deductible (check with your tax specialist yearly). Be aware of the fact that you will have to pay an origination fee anywhere from $75 to several hundred dollars, plus the cost of an appraisal and title insurance. So count the cost to be sure it is worth it.

- **Refinancing/Home** This is sometimes referred to as a "cash-out" refinancing option. This is where the property owner refinances the entire loan for more than the property is worth and uses the extra cash to pay off credit cards. Once again, you face the same temptation to use *some* (just a little bit, not much) of the surplus cash on luxury items rather than paying off debt. The primary disadvantage to this approach is that you are stretching your mortgage over 15 or 30 years. The total interest cost over three decades can wind up being pretty large, so you would need to keep two things in mind: (1) you would do this only once, and (2) you need to concentrate on paying down the mortgage by paying extra every month toward the principal, thereby shaving as much as a decade's worth of interest off your loan.

- **Refinancing/Car** This is a secured loan and you can borrow on it—but be careful! You need to calculate whether you will run out of *car* before you run out of car *debt*. If the answer is yes to that question, then this is not your best option. It's very difficult to buy a new car when you owe more than the car is worth.

- **Terms** This is one of the easiest ways to lower your payments. Just pick up the phone and call the credit card company and tell them you are looking to consolidate your loans though another lending institution if you can't get the interest rate down on the card you currently have. You'd be surprised at how many customer service representatives are authorized to lower the interest rates right there on the phone for you (without having to call over their supervisor). It's worth ten minutes of your time to save anywhere from several hundred to several thousand dollars!

- **Personal Loans** This is an option only for those who have undamaged credit and who would qualify for an unsecured loan. The interest rates could be in the low double digits, which isn't as low as some of the other options, but the advantage is that they are usually less interest than the 20 percent plus you are now paying the credit card company.

- **The Good Old Standbys** I've already mentioned CCCS (Consumer Credit Counseling Services) several times by now. But they are different from the for-profit debt consolidation companies in that their services are free (and confidential). Since there are branches all over the country, they are as close as your Yellow Pages. You can also apply for their low-rate mortgage program. They will negotiate the lower fees with the lending institutions. Their initial consultations usually last an hour (by phone or in person) to help you decide if you even need a debt management plan. In order to use their services, you are required to fill out a form that details all your expenses. They walk you through the eye-opening experience of seeing these stretched out over the course of a year (most of us budget monthly and only review those figures). They'll even tell you if you can pay off your debt without their help. Or, you can try 1-800-4 DEBT HELP, and in some cases there's no interest if you qualify for the "Good payer program."

The Seven Rights (Will Help Fix the Wrong)

As you navigate your way from financial bondage to freedom, it's important to know your "debtor's rights"— especially as you begin to dialogue with credit card companies and financial counselors. Here they are in their simplest form:

1. You have a right to know what your credit report says about you. The lender looks at this file every time you apply for credit. Employers and insurance companies can even request and review this form.

2. You have a right to a complete and accurate report. If the report is not correct, you have the right to ask the credit bureau to fix it. Of course, this may feel like getting a bill passed into law, but it's your right. The Fair Credit Reporting Act says both creditors and credit bureaus must investigate reports of erroneous material, and if an error is found, they must report the correction to all three bureaus.

3. You have the right to a fresh start. Negative information must be erased from your file after seven years and a bankruptcy after eight years.

4. You have the right to know who has seen your file. If adverse action has been taken, you have the right to know about it. The full name and contact info of the company that asked for your report must be given.

5. You have the right to give your side of the situation or dispute. If you state that some of your information has been reported in error, but the creditor disagrees and refuses to remove it from your file, you have the right to ask for your side of the dispute to be attached to your file. You should keep concise records for this reason.

6. You have the right to confidentiality. It seems contradictory when you have so many different agencies that may be given access to your file. These authorized agencies have the right to review your file, but others, such as a former spouse or lawyers for litigation purposes, do not. This is another reason why you should request a list of who has seen your files.

7. You have the right to sue the credit bureau. This is a "right" but it is not one I would recommend. It is often costly to sue them and difficult (if not impossible) to win.

Massage Therapy

Long before I met my husband, back when I was an insurance broker working full time and making a good living, I had my very first massage. The LMT (Licensed Massage Therapist) was part of the "Deluxe Package" at our local health club. It was great! I only had to tip her $5 (this was many years ago, and it was a good tip; most people tipped her $3), and I got an hour's worth of relaxation!

I still budget a trip to the LMT a couple of times every month, and it's worth every penny. It's amazing how rubbing the right place makes your sore muscles feel better and tight shoulders relax (I'm going tomorrow after sitting at this computer for eight hours today). It makes my tension disappear.

It's also amazing how "massaging" your debt, bit by bit, can make it eventually disappear. The following points are small but significant things you can do to eliminate credit card debt. If you do just one of these per week, you'll have a new financial outlook within three months.

Face the Facts

A critical part of assessing your situation is to list and assess this information on columnar paper. Take the credit report that you ordered from one of our previous exercises and use it as an information source for the following:

- Creditors
- Balance on each account
- Minimum payment
- Number of payments left
- Interest rate
- Due date

Once this information has been documented in one place, it will be easier to ascertain your true debt load and develop a systematic plan to get out of debt. This is something that you can do at home or have CCCS do in their offices.

Cut Costs

The most effective thing you can do is to reduce your committed expenses (the lowest level on the financial pyramid in chapter 4). For right now, focus on those monthly expenses that are not fixed (unlike mortgage and car payments). But it's not enough to cut costs if you're not committed to applying these savings to credit card debt. The savings will just be absorbed into spending elsewhere unless you have a plan and earmark these cuts to go to specific debt. The ideas in my bestselling book *Shop, Save, and Share,* as well as my second book, *How to Save Money Every Day,* have helped thousands of families cut costs and get out of debt. There are more specific ideas in this area later in this book.

A more dramatic approach would be to reduce your fixed expenses by trading down in a home and/or car in order to get out of debt. This is an issue that you will need to decide based on your specific situation and the severity of your financial condition. There's more information on this topic in chapter 7.

It's not enough to cut costs if you're not committed to applying these savings to credit card debt.

Credit Cards

How do you know if you are getting a good value for your credit cards? You want a card that charges a low rate (not merely a temporary introductory rate), no annual fee, and one with a fixed rate (not subject to increase).

Don't be deceived by some of the "reward" cards, either—do the math on those cards. For example, most cards that offer frequent-flier-miles require that you earn 25,000 miles (at one mile per dollar, = $25,000 spent) in order to buy *one* ticket (which averages $250 to $300). This means you are earning one cent for every dollar you spend. These reward cards also subliminally encourage you to overspend on your credit card.

For a list of credit cards by category (low-rate, no annual fee, etc.), go to *www.bankrate.com* or *www. cardtrak.com*. Other tools available to help you get the card that is right for you are *www.getsmart.com* or *www.creditcardgoodies.com*.

Paying Down the Principal

I am a mom who wanted to stay home with her children, and I developed a plan to do so. My plan was based on solid principles and some of my great-grandma's commonsense strategies.

While I do believe that there is "wisdom in many counselors," such as financial counselors, we don't have to overpay for advice. Much of the best advice is free (on the Internet) or compiled nicely into an inexpensive book such as the one you are reading.

You can buy an expensive "pay down kit" from a financial planner, or you can follow some simple steps and watch your debts diminish. Here are a couple of strategies to pay down the principal rather than merely managing the interest:

- *Pay the original minimum on each credit entry from our "Face the Facts" section above.* If you continue to pay the amount of the *original* minimum payment, you will soon find that the required minimum is reduced. If your payment remains at the higher amount, you are paying on the principal and saving on interest by paying the debt off early.

- *Pay the least first or the most first.* Are you confused? It's best to organize your debts in one of two ways: (1) the highest interest rate and (2) the shortest pay-off time as the top priorities on the list. If all the payoff figures are close, then pay the one with the highest interest rate. However, if you have a much smaller note at a lower interest rate, it tends to serve as a morale booster to go ahead and get it paid off, and then apply the total amount of that payment to the next bill on your list. For example, if you have a card on which you owe $1,500 at 20 percent and another on which you owe only $200 at 18 percent, go ahead and pay off the small debt first as a boost to your ego.

Rebuilding Good Credit

A bankruptcy will stay on your credit report at least eight years. Even when you've rebuilt credit after this severe kind of damage, you won't be able to qualify for rock-bottom mortgage rates. According to Jean Sherman Chatzky, financial editor at *USA Weekend Magazine* (January 21, 2000), these are the things that will have to be done to rebuild credit:

- *Close accounts you don't use.* To lenders, charge accounts or home-equity lines of credit mean you could go on a spending spree at any time.
- *Don't hit all your credit limits.* If you're using 80 percent or more of your available credit, it's a sign to

lenders that you're overextended.

- *Limit inquiries into your credit record.* Minimize the number of times you apply for credit, because each inquiry will appear on your credit report, whether you get the credit or not. Keep in mind that all inquiries for one purpose, such as a mortgage, will count as one.

- *Don't miss payments.* Automate as many payments as possible if you can keep up with these automated payments in your accounts at home. If you make sure the funds are there, you will never be late on payments. Everyone from health clubs to electric companies has these services available.

You've made it to the end of this chapter, and hopefully you are motivated to get out there and hit the pavement! Remember that if a woman who steals her child's french fries, has had $40,000 of debt, and freezes her credit cards can become debt free—so can you!

❧ seven ❧
Movin' On Up
*Mortgages/Biting Off More
Than You Can Chew*

Your home is supposed to be a haven for you and your family. It's a place where you can (allegedly) have privacy—except for moms. As soon as a mom wants to take a shower or dry her hair, her entire family seems to have a question that only Mom can answer or a crisis that only Mom can solve. My own children ask such urgent questions as:

"MOM! HEY, MOM! WE'RE OUT OF PEANUT BUTTER! WHAT AM I GOING TO HAVE FOR LUNCH?" (And it's only ten in the morning.)

Or Joshua pounds on the door and yells:

"MAMA! CAN I HAVE NICHOLAS AND MATTHEW SPEND THE NIGHT FOR MY BIRTHDAY PARTY?" (His birthday is in September and it's currently December.)

Or my kids give me a blow-by-blow description of a crisis through the bathroom door: "Mom, Jonathan dripped the red candle wax on the carpet!" (Here's a little tip: You should *never* ask the child *why* they were playing with the wax in the candle because it will only lead to frustration as they give you reasons like: (1) I didn't *know* I wasn't supposed to play with candle wax, (2) I was helping you move it to a safe place, or (3) It's not my fault; Daniel made me do it.

Instead, it's best to get a brown grocery bag, place it over the wax, set the iron on medium low, and gently iron it until the wax comes up.)

Or, my personal favorite (which usually happens after an entire morning of questions and crises when I've finally yelled at them to leave me alone so I can take a shower) is:

"MOM, THE PASTOR'S WIFE IS STANDING IN THE ENTRYWAY AND WANTS TO TALK TO YOU WHEN YOU'RE DONE YELLING AT US!"

Home is supposed to be a safe place despite all the frustrations of a busy family. It is a place that we want to invest in emotionally, physically, and financially. But what if that safe place is violated?

When I was twelve years old, we went on a family vacation, traveling from Texas to Indiana. We were gone two weeks, and when we came back, we discovered to our horror that our home had been plundered from top to bottom. The thieves stole the television, stereo equipment, photographic equipment, my mom's heirloom jewelry from Spain (it was gorgeous!), and even the pennies from my bank! They went through every drawer and closet—nothing was safe from their greedy hands. We discovered "new" missing things for months to come.

Knowing that the thieves had been in my room, through my closets and drawers, gave me nightmares for months. What if they come back? What will I find missing next? Is anything really mine if someone can break in and take it away from me?

Here's the final twist to the story: the perpetrator, or head of the group that broke into our home, wasn't a gang member, felon, or professional criminal. It was a family member.

Maybe you've never been robbed, but you are vulnerable to a kind of theft that could rob you of your ability to secure a mortgage loan, which would greatly impact your home and family life. Perpetrators of this kind of theft may even be a family member or someone you know. It could cause you countless hours of labor and thousands of dollars to recover from it. It's called identity theft.

You may be wondering why I'm beginning this chapter by discussing identity theft, and it is because it is a very real threat to your credit rating. Some 500,000 to 700,000 Americans a year are at risk of having their identities stolen, according to government and private sector estimates.

What is identity theft? According to America's Community Bankers: "Identity theft occurs when someone steals your personal information and uses it to establish credit, borrow money, charge items, or even commit crimes in your name."

After I explain how to protect yourself from identity theft, we will discuss the following in the rest of this chapter: (1) "Five Do's and Don'ts From Mortgage Experts," (2) "Don't Move Up, Don't Move Down, Just Move Over," and (3) "The Principle of the Thirteenth Payment."

Quick Facts on Identity Theft

- The U.S. Federal Trade Commission says that identity theft is the number one source of consumer complaints, comprising 42 percent of all complaints in 2001.

- According to *www.CBSnews.com*, every seventy-nine seconds a thief steals someone's identity, opens accounts in the victim's name, and goes on a buying spree.

- The Gartner Group, a technology research group, warns that there is likely to be "mass victimization" of consumers within the next two years (December 2002).

- The July 2000 issue of *Consumer Reports* cited a study where 50 percent of the credit reports checked contained errors. (There are two main reasons errors may appear on your credit report. One is that you have been mistaken for another person with a similar name and their information ends up in your file. The other more serious cause is identity fraud.)

- Credit card fraud hits one in twenty users, and identity theft hit one in fifty during the past year (Gartner, Inc., *msnbc.com/new/718115.asp?cp1=1*).

- Identity theft costs the average victim more than $1,000 to repair the resulting damage, according to the Federal Trade Commission.

- According to the FTC's figures, identity theft is the most popular form of consumer fraud, in part because it is the most profitable. Identity thieves stole nearly $100 million from financial institutions last year, or an average of $6,767 per victim (FTC, 2002).

The experts agree that while the incidence of Internet identity theft is growing, you are still more likely to become a victim of this federal crime by a more traditional means, such as improperly discarding credit card or other financial data. Without trying to be paranoid, sometimes this theft can occur through your kids' friends, a local merchant, or even a family member. I know of one mother who was well educated and appeared to be an upstanding citizen but had, in fact, an unhealthy obsession with spending money. When her credit problems became so great and her payment history so poor that she couldn't even get a phone, she used her teenage daughter's social security number and began to ruin *her* credit history, as well!

But there's no need to become unduly alarmed. There are some tips that can help you avoid identity theft and help you to deal with the situation if you were to become a victim.

Protect Your Identity

- **Unsolicited Requests** Never respond to these requests for your social security number (SSN) or financial data.
- **Shred It!** For less than $20, you can purchase a shredder. Before you discard credit card information, ATM receipts, and any pre-approved credit offers you have received (i.e., credit card junk mail), shred them.
- **Statements** Check all credit card and bank statements for accuracy on a regular basis.
- **Checks** Never put your social security number on your checks. When you order checks, consider having them mailed to your place of business or, if you're home during the day, to your door (via FedEx

or UPS) instead of your mailbox (assuming you don't have a secure/locked mailbox). Mailbox theft is on the rise in many areas. A friend recently had her checks stolen from her mailbox, and the thieves wrote thousands of dollars of checks before she realized what had happened. She is still in the process of working with police and the bank to try to prove she should not be held responsible for nearly $10,000 worth of stolen checks. You may need to shop around for a check company that will ship checks to your door. Some will only mail the first box by FedEx and the rest of the order by regular mail (i.e., their rush service), which doesn't help prevent theft. One company that does offer this option is Checks in the Mail (*www.citm.com*). The police also warned this friend not to put outgoing bills in her own mailbox. Thieves can steal those checks, use a special wash to remove the ink, and rewrite the checks for their own use.

- **PIN Codes** Make sure these are not based on your name, date of birth, or other easy-to-figure-out codes.

- **Credit Reports** We've already recommended that you obtain these reports; in this case you need to check it for accuracy. For easy access, I'll list them again: Equifax (*www.equifax.com*) at (800) 685-1111; Experian (*www.experian.com*) (888) 397-3742; Trans Union (*www.tuc.com*) (800) 888-4213.

- **Secure Sites** If the Internet source you are ordering from does not offer a secure page, do not enter any credit information. Secure sites begin with "https," and your software will usually show a closed lock or key to indicate security.

- **Online Purchases** Be sure to pay for these with a credit card in order to assure you get what you paid for and to limit your liability. You have more recourse with a credit card than you do by paying with a check.
- **SSN** Be very careful when giving out your social security information. Every year you should order a copy of your "Earnings and Benefits" statement directly from the Social Security Administration at (800) 772-1213.

If You Become a Victim

If you find that you have become a victim of identity theft, take the following actions immediately:

- **Police** File a formal police report.
- **Banker** Notify all of your bankers of the theft.
- **Financial Contacts** Notify all people with whom you have a financial relationship in any capacity (business partners, financial institutions, employer, etc.).
- **Tag Accounts** You must request that all accounts (credit card, etc.) closed due to fraud be tagged "Closed at the consumer's request." Otherwise, it could appear that a creditor shut down your account, and this will reflect negatively on your credit report.
- **Credit Bureaus** Notify the three main credit bureau fraud units of your identity theft. They are: Equifax (*www.equifax.com*) at (800) 525-6285; Experian (*www.experian.com*) (888) 397-3742; Trans Union (*www.tuc.com*) (800) 680-7289.
- **Passwords** Establish a password for telephone inquiries on credit card accounts.

- **Alert** Place a fraud alert statement on your credit report if you have become a victim; it will alert creditors to the fact that your financial identity has been compromised.
- **Check Theft** If the thief has access to your checking account, report it to the appropriate agency: Check Rite (800) 766-2748; Chexsystems (800) 428-9623; CrossCheck (707) 586-0551; Equifax (800) 437-5120; National Processing Co. and SCAN (800) 526-5380; TeleCheck (800) 710-9898.
- **Bi-Monthly Copies** Request bi-monthly copies of your credit report until your case is resolved; these are *free* to fraud victims.
- **Post Office** Check with the post office for unauthorized change of address requests.
- **Follow-up** Send all of your contacts (see above) letters and keep copies of all correspondence.

Remain Alert

You should suspect identity theft if you are denied credit for no apparent reason. Or if routine financial statements stop arriving in a timely manner. For the most updated information about identity theft and how to avoid it, go to:

- **Federal Trade Commission** *www.consumer.gov/idtheft*
- **Americans for Consumer Education and Competition** *www.acecusa.org/tips/*
- **The Privacy Council** *www.privacycouncil.com/links=optout.htm*

Movin' On Up

You may still be wondering why I opened a chapter on mortgages and owning a home with an entire section on identity theft.

To confuse the reader?

No.

To fill space?

Um . . . uh . . . no.

To show you a creative way to take someone else's credit rating and retire to Bora Bora?

Definitely not!

To point out how important it is to be alert about this very real problem so that you will not have problems in acquiring a mortgage?

Bingo!

Five Do's and Don'ts From Mortgage Experts

If you want to maximize your ability to get a good mortgage rate and qualify for that dream house you have in mind, there are some very practical ways for you to get there from here. One practical way, according to Brian Israel, vice-president of Chicago-based Harris Trust and Savings Bank's residential mortgage division, is "Number one, pay your bills on time. There is no single element that can so dramatically impact the success of an application as your credit history. Another thing, of course, is savings. People should have a good disciplined savings pattern. That's the kind of behavior that's going to make them a successful homeowner" (Michael Larson, *www.moneycentral.msn.com/articles/*

banking/, 2002). Here are some more of the do's and don'ts from the experts.

Please Do:

- **Make On-Time Debt Payments** This may sound mundane in its simplicity, but if you are saving toward a home and run into a difficult financial season, pay your credit cards before you pay your light bill if you want to qualify for a mortgage someday. Every thirty-, sixty-, or ninety-day delinquency on a loan or credit card is going to reduce the credit score on your report. This is a consideration the loan officer will have to take into account when approving your mortgage and the amount of the loan.

- **If You Have to Miss Something . . .** If you are laid off work, have a physical illness, or some other unforeseen situation arises where you cannot pay your bills and you are going to have to miss a loan payment of some kind, be strategic in choosing that missed payment. You should miss the credit card payment first, followed by the payment on any installment loan you might have, and finally the payment for an existing mortgage. According to Michael Larsen, a writer for MSN Money, "That's because credit-scoring systems look at the performance of similar loans first when deciding what type of score to assign. It will give the most weight to the performance of another mortgage, for example, and then the performance of something like an auto loan, which features fixed payments and a fixed rate the way many mortgages do."

- **Pay Off Debt** It's important to pay off as many

smaller debts as you can so that when you go to apply for a mortgage, you will have a better chance at getting a good rate. Even if you end up putting down a smaller amount at closing and end up with a larger mortgage, you will be better off than with the high-interest rates of most consumer debt. If you're pursuing paying down debt, then you are in good company. Larry Hamilton, executive officer of South Trust's mortgage lending division in Birmingham, Alabama, says that consumers are "putting less equity in their homes, borrowing more against their homes, and they're paying off consumer debt."

- **Mortgage Takes Priority** If you have a new job and the means to secure multiple loans (such as a mortgage, new car, and new credit cards), secure the mortgage loan first. Whenever your credit is scored, each application for credit becomes a liability to your rating. Numerous credit inquiries, such as these, can hurt your overall credit score, especially if they are filed in the months prior to the mortgage loan review process.
- **Save, Save, Save** It is best to increase the size of the down payment you're able to make by saving as much as possible. Invest these savings in secure accounts that offer reasonable rates of return, automatic payroll deductions, or other financial incentives to save. In chapter 6, we talked about six sources of income that could be applied toward paying down debt. Once you've paid off consumer debt, apply these toward your savings for a down payment on your next house. For quick review, they are:
  - Inheritance

- Income tax refund
- Overtime
- Bonus
- Insurance dividend refund
- Pay raise
- Any other unexpected additional income

Five Don'ts

- **Avoid Big Purchases** If you have to get a loan for a large purchase, such as a $15,000 auto loan, it could prevent you from qualifying for the mortgage amount you want. Lenders do not look favorably at adding debt upon debt. Besides that, the more money you are spending on loans, the less you will have to put toward a mortgage. The best car to drive is usually the paid-for car that you are driving now—especially if it translates into a better home for your family. "Generally, as a rule of thumb, you will want your total debt obligation, including mortgage, to be no more than 36 percent of your gross monthly income," says South Trust's Hamilton. "You certainly don't want to load up on consumer debt if you're anticipating purchasing a home and you're unsure of what your mortgage payment is going to be, and if you think you're within the range of exceeding that 36 percent requirement."

- **Live Within Your Means** In some ways, obtaining a mortgage is like gambling if you do not know how credit ratings are scored, how much of a loan your family income will support, and how much your new mortgage payment will be compared to your existing one. For example, if you shoot for a loan that would raise your payments from $500 in rent to a whopping $1,600 per month principle/interest/insurance payment, then you are likely to experience what the industry calls "payment shock." A lender will look at this differential, and you will find yourself in one of two situations: (1) you won't qualify for the loan, or (2) you will end up having to cover too much loan with too little money. A final note in this section is to point out that if you are turned down for a mortgage loan because you're trying to buy too much house, it will be indicated as a huge negative on your credit rating. Then when you go to apply for a lower mortgage loan, you already have this additional strike against you. It is far better to own your house than to have your house own you.

It is far better to own your house than to have your house own you.

- **Pre-Qualified Versus Pre-Approved** When you are pre-qualified for a loan, you are basically given an estimate of how much of a loan you will qualify for after you've submitted income, credit, and debt information. Michael D. Larson says, "In this case, the lender does not pull credit reports, check debt to income ratios, and perform other underwriting steps. But by getting pre-approved, these latter steps are performed and you are that much closer to obtaining a loan and locking in a rate and term. The first is an estimate, the latter is much closer to the final product."

- **Money Personalities** In chapter 2, we discussed different kinds of money personalities. Don't forget this when it comes to getting a mortgage loan. If you take out a thirty-year fixed-rate loan rather than a fifteen-year mortgage and invest the money saved on monthly payments, you might earn a higher return on your money in the long run. But few money personalities have this kind of discipline. If you are the kind of personality that spends any extra money you have, then it would be better to get the shorter term, which will force you to invest your money toward paying off your house in a shorter amount of time.

- **Hidden Burdens** Don't forget the "extras" involved in home ownership. You will have to cover short-term and long-term repairs and maintenance: when something breaks you will pay to have it repaired or replaced. On the financial side of the equation, don't forget that home ownership brings the additional responsibility of greater financial accountability. For example, missing a rent payment carries a much smaller penalty than defaulting on a loan. You could quickly find yourself in a higher-interest bracket when it comes to the credit card offers you receive in the mail. Larson says, "Too many black marks on the financial history and it will be 23 percent interest credit card mailers that show up in the mailbox rather than the 9.9 percent ones your neighbor gets."

Don't Move Up, Don't Move Down, Just Move Over

When I was on the *Simplify Your Life* television reality series, one of the families I worked with was combining two households for a "yours, mine, and ours" family. In considering where they would live and what their monthly expenses would be, I helped them come to the conclusion that "moving over" was best. The "American Dream" seems to be that we have to "move up" in order to arrive in life. But if your house owns you instead of the other way around, how is that high living? On the other hand, who wants to "move down" to a lower house payment that may require you to move into a smaller, older, or less adequate home? That's why I came up with a third option: "move over."

This family that I worked with in the television series was serious about wanting Mom to stay home with the baby they were expecting (theirs). But between child-support payments (his) and the expenses of another child that lived with them (hers), they had to make a move. They were living in a dream house that was in a brand-new neighborhood and had a gorgeous view of a forest in their backyard. They moved to an equal-sized house (which they needed) that was in a slightly older but quaint neighborhood and lowered their mortgage payments enough for Mom to stay home with the newborn. It wasn't easy, but it was the optimum choice for their objectives. In the long run, they are in a much better position to save for a down payment on their *next* mortgage (by the time their family outgrows their present house).

Sometimes contentment lies in how you view your situation and what you are willing to trade for those things that matter most in life.

The Principle of the Thirteenth Payment

Look at your original mortgage loan and see how little of your initial payments go toward the principal.

You are mainly servicing the interest. But if you add enough "extra" to your regular payment each month to constitute a thirteenth payment every twelve months, you could shave off a significant portion of your mortgage. When you shop for a mortgage, keep this thirteenth payment in mind and *do not* choose a mortgage company that charges a penalty for paying off your loan early! What if you already have a mortgage with this type of penalty? Don't worry, the savings for paying it off early will probably be greater than the penalty—but you won't save as much as you might have saved.

If you want precise amounts and the exact timing on how to pay your mortgage in half the time, you can invest in a financial calculator (available at electronics stores), or you could contact a volunteer financial counselor. Or, you can find these online tools at sites such as *www.interest.com/hugh/calc/mort.html* or *www.mortgageselect.com/calculators.asp?referrer62* or *http://homeadvisor.msn.com/financing/financing overview.aspx.*

One family I was working with went to the second calculator, which asks the question, "Should I pay more on the principal?" They were shown that if they paid $66 per month extra against their principal, their mortgage would go from thirty years to twenty-four and they would save $45,000 in interest payments. Look at the bottom line: twenty-four years of $66 per month is $19,000 compared to $45,000 in interest! It takes so little to save so much.

There are several ways you can make this thirteenth payment. Pick the one that best meets your needs as well as your money personality.

- **Biweekly Mortgage** Some banks are currently offering this option, but I believe it's best to get a regular monthly mortgage and then go ahead and make the biweekly payments on your own. That way you are not legally locked into this payment schedule should you have a financial setback. This plan is where you make half of your mortgage payment every two weeks. You will automatically end up making the thirteenth payment in that year. This plan is great for people who get paid every two weeks.

- **Independent Service Bureau** This is a company that offers to set up your biweekly payment plans. They take the money out of your savings or checking account every two weeks, and once they have a full month's mortgage payment, they send it to your mortgage company. Some mortgage companies also do this. But be careful, some of these service bureaus will charge a setup or initiation fee of anywhere from $300 to $400, as well as a transaction fee every time they collect money. So if you're looking for this plan through your mortgage company, be sure that there is no initiation fee and that the transaction fees are nominal.

- **Automatic Payment Plans** You may want to set up a deduction from your paycheck that goes directly to your mortgage company or to a biweekly mortgage payment plan. The advantage to this is that you will never see the money, and if your family tends to spend whatever they have in the checkbook, this is a proactive way to force you to invest in your home and pay down that mortgage.

- **Just Pay More** If you do not want to subscribe to a structured payment plan, just send in a little extra every month, telling your mortgage company that this extra is to go toward the principal. In the long run, if you're diligent, you may save even more than the thirteenth payment.

- **Advantages/Disadvantages** The primary advantage to the thirteenth payment principle is that you are avoiding years of interest and a big chunk of change. Even if you sell your house before you pay off the loan (as most people do), you will still be putting more money toward your equity, which you will get back as soon as the house is sold (unless you sell your home at a loss). The only disadvantage to this is that you will eventually lose the tax benefit of writing off the interest and other possible tax deductions. But the only time that disadvantage will outweigh the benefits of paying off the loan early is for someone with a unique tax situation, such as someone who owns rental property and needs the write-off. Check with your tax consultant if you fit this category.

———

The last thought I'd like to leave you with in this chapter has to do with your home—not your house. As a military family who moved twelve times in thirteen years, we learned that home is where our family is—not the physical dwelling that we live in. Sure, we want a nice, big, spacious place to call our own, but we can learn to be content in a smaller one if our family is together. Your kids will always remember your home as bigger than what it was (remember the first time you visited your childhood home as an adult after a long absence?). But even more than that, they'll remember what happened between the walls that you called home. Professor Emmett Brown said in *Back to the Future*,

"Your future is what you make of it—so make it a good one." I agree with a slight modification: "God has a bright future planned for you—so let Him make it a good one."

eight

Cash for Trash

I had just finished two grueling days of taping on the South Jersey shore area for the new reality TV series called *Simplify Your Life*. As I mentioned, this show brought in experts to help solve an average family's problems, and I addressed the family's financial concerns. The family I worked with seemed so typical that when I began this book, I patterned the fictional "Bensons" you met in chapter 1 after this real-life family.

After a successful shoot, the production assistant graciously offered to drive me to a nearby beach amusement park for some R&R. So, still in my business suit and heels, she and I headed toward the boardwalk to get fresh pretzels and see the rides.

We had the thrill of riding on an ancient wooden roller coaster that went above the boardwalk and over the ocean. Then we saw a "Bungee Flying" ride. A young woman was being hoisted up 300 feet in a harness. When they gave her the thumbs-up, she pulled a rip cord and fell from that height until a bungee cord caught her and she bounced up another 100 feet. The ride made her look like Super Girl flying through the sky—except most superheroes don't scream at the top of their lungs.

When I saw that ride, this conservative mother of seven said, "I've got to try that!" When I told the young woman who drove me what I was going to do, she gave me a look that said, "Are you nuts or something?"

But the only question she actually uttered was "Are you going to do that in heels?"

Yes, I was. And I did.

The only thing that concerned me was that when I was hoisted up three hundred feet and the ground was getting farther and farther away—my harness started slipping. I wondered how my newfound friend would break the news to my husband. But alas, the harness held, the rip cord pulled, and the adventure began!

I went free falling three hundred feet, and the ground rushed up so quickly that my stomach ended up in my throat. It was frightening and exhilarating at the same time.

I look at life as an adventure—especially when it comes to stretching dollars and being a good financial steward of the resources God has given me. But if we're not careful, we can find our resources dwindling and sound stewardship slipping further and further out of our grasp.

To reach our goal of spending less than we make, sometimes we need to have the ultimate adventure—earning more by turning our trash into cash and paying less for the items we buy. There are three simple ways to do this: buying and selling via online auctions, consignment stores, and garage sales! Paying a dime on the dollar for a product still in its original box that you'd pay full price for at Stuff Mart is a great thrill. Not only do these methods simplify your life by helping you de-clutter, but they also provide a way to keep more change in your pocket if you can learn how to navigate them wisely.

Garage Sales

Tips for Buyers

- **Stay on Budget** Garage sales need to be a part of your monthly budget. We usually budget $50 a week. This covers even the major garage sale purchases in the long run. The garage-sale benefit greatly diminishes if you go over budget to "save money."
- ***Do* Leave Home Without It** If you're one given to impulse buying, leave your checkbook and wallet in the car. While you're walking back to your vehicle to get your money, you'll have time to think about your purchase and decide whether you really need it or not.

Tips for Sellers

Here are my top ten tips to hosting a successful garage sale. If you follow them wisely, you'll find yourself flying high—without the bungee cord!

- **Collect** Throughout the year, throw stuff in a big box marked "Garage Sale." Not only will you relieve clutter, you'll soon have enough diverse items to host a sale.
- **Location** You may want to buddy up with a friend whose house has a better location to catch the attention of drive-by traffic. Or, ask a neighbor (or two)

if you could host their sales together with your own—you could get three times the garage sale traffic with combined sales.

- **Advertise** Use brightly colored poster board and a good contrasting color like blue or yellow. Keep the lettering brief and legible and tape some balloons to the sign.
- **Pricing** If you price your product, you are more likely to sell it. Most people don't want to keep asking, "How much for this?" Although there will still be some who will try to barter with you on the price, that's to be expected. Begin pricing items weeks before the sale, placing them in a "finished" pile in your garage.
- **Cash** Have at least $20 in coins, twenty one-dollar bills, and four five-dollar bills. Keep your money box in a safe location and never leave it unattended. Bring each $100 earned into your house for safe-keeping.
- **Checks** Never take a check from someone you don't know. This isn't just a matter of trust, it's one of stewardship. Most people know to bring cash.

Never take a check from someone you don't know. This isn't just a matter of trust, it's one of stewardship.

- **Hold** Never hold an item without a substantial non-refundable deposit. Otherwise, it is likely that the customer will not return and you will have lost your opportunity to sell it.

- **Marketing** Place furniture and bikes that will draw attention by the curb where people can see them. Try marketing ideas such as "buy three books/get three free." It's amazing how well this works—people really respond to the word *free*!
- **Clean** Run sturdy plastic toys through the dishwasher, spot clean the armchair, and polish wood furniture—it's worth it! If an item looks newer simply because it's clean, you'll be able to get as much as 50 percent *more* for it.
- **Expand** Let your kids get in on the action by selling lemonade on hot days or coffee and doughnuts on cool mornings. Be sure they understand how to make change and how to be courteous to customers. Who knows? They may earn enough to fund their college education (or at least buy a new bike)!

Consignment Stores

Tips for Buyers

The main benefit of shopping at consignment stores, compared to garage sales, is that you don't have to haggle over a price. Also, the selection is often nicer (since stores are pickier about what they will sell) and better organized, making it easier to find what you need.

- **Look and See** Before you buy anything at a consignment store, look it over very carefully and make sure it is in good condition.
- **Check Back Often** The selection changes frequently, so check back often. Some stores will even offer to call you when a certain item becomes available.

Tips for Sellers

The benefit of selling your things to a consignment store vs. an online auction is that you don't have to package and mail the item. It's a one-time drop-off and then you get a check. Here's a checklist for successful consigning:

- **Non-Traditional** Most people think that you can only consign clothing, but there are all kinds of these stores popping up in our communities. Sporting equipment, cars, furniture, and even appliances can be consigned in some areas. *Play It Again Sports* was a great place to get rid of Bob's "old" racquetball racquet when he upgraded to the latest and greatest model. Check the Yellow Pages under the topic of your choice and see if there is a "used" section—call these used vendors and ask if they allow consignments. Sometimes you have not because you ask not.

- **Top Quality** Just as in garage sales, you will need to have your items in top-notch condition in order to get the best price. Some clothing consignment places require that you dry-clean the item before you bring it in. In this case, it's important to do your research first: you don't want to pay $6 to have a dress dry-cleaned that will bring you only $8, less the 20 percent consignment fee. You don't want to work to break even—you want to make a profit! Which brings us to our next critical point.

- **Fees** This "detail" could make the difference of hundreds of dollars each year. Some stores charge as much as a 50 percent consignment fee while others charge as little as 15 percent. Do your research (on the phone).

EBay and other Online Auctions

In 2002 there were over 100,000 people who made their living full time on eBay—and that number is on the rise. You can make a lot of money, and you can get some incredibly good deals if you know the ins and outs of this resource. Kari Ilg is a new mom who works full time as an engineer out of her home, with an occasional business trip. She makes money on eBay on a part-time basis. She says she makes her family's extra spending money online, which can vary depending on how much time is invested. "This is my fun job because it gives me a break from my stress job," says Kari. One of the ways you can make even more on eBay is if you set yourself up as a wholesaler for a particular product. In Kari's case, she is a wholesaler for Boyd's Bears Company. So she makes even more money by buying these at wholesale and selling them near retail.

In addition to a wholesale business, you could sell off your excess household goods, clothing, and other products and get more for them than you would at a garage sale, so it would be worth your time. You may be pleasantly surprised at the value a potential bidder might place on what you may call a castoff and they call a collectible. Some industrious people even routinely shop at garage sales and antique stores for the express purpose of reselling items at a considerable profit on eBay. But it's important to count the costs of your time and effort.

The minimum that Kari will ask for an item is $5 for a piece of clothing or other product. "Otherwise," she says, "it just isn't worth it to me." She recently sold everything in her bathroom for over $200 by selling in lots and individually. She strategically tied in the matching products from one eBay site to another and ended up selling everything to only two different buyers. She was able to redecorate her entire bathroom from the proceeds. She buys all her Christmas gifts on eBay, making sure that items are new and in the box. This engineering young mom's goal is to eventually quit her primary job and sell enough on eBay to make up the difference in the family's budget.

Other avid eBay enthusiasts include Jeremy and Cleis Jordan, a retired couple who own the *Casa de Patron* historic bed and breakfast in Lincoln, New Mexico, where Billy the Kid once slept (*www. casapatron.com*). Currently, they buy and sell specialty items such as antique washboards, soaps, and related ephemera. In a research interview for this chapter, Jeremy said, "Cleis even finds old photos of the Lincoln County area. There is just no telling what someone out there is passionate about."

Here are some tips from these experts, and others, to keep in mind whether you are buying or selling:

Tips for Buyers

- **History** The first thing you should check when you're buying online is the seller's history. If others were not happy with this seller, then chances are you won't be, either!
- **Final Costs** If a seller doesn't list the postage, handling, and insurance costs, then be sure to ask this. "I know someone who bought an item for $10 and then had to pay $35 for shipping, which wasn't revealed at the time of the sale—and in that case it wasn't worth it," says Kari.
- **Research** Before you purchase an item, be sure to do your research and find that same product else-

where on the Internet. You may only think you're getting a good deal because it's on eBay and then end up spending twice as much as you should have! This is how sellers make their money—but you don't want it to be at your expense.

- **Experience** Before you begin selling online, first buy several things so you can gain this experience. Once you start selling, you are subject to a rating system, in which the buyer rates you, and this rating is then posted online. You want to keep the best rating possible, and you'll need to gain the experience of buying online to see what makes for a contented buyer. Ask yourself: Why did I buy this item? What did I like about the seller's service? Once you answer these questions, you'll be on your way to knowing how to make a good sale and a happy customer.

Tips for Sellers

- **Online Fees** When you're selling, be sure to add up all the fees that are involved for the online site and figure that into your asking price. The first fee is a *listing fee,* anywhere from 25¢ to $2, depending upon the starting price of your item. The *selling fee* is a percentage based on the final selling price. The final fee to eBay is an *online fee* when you accept an online payment (usually around 1 percent).

- **Photo** Invest in a good digital camera. The photo of the item is one of the most important selling points. In fact, a photo is mandatory for many buyers. Multiple images are often worthwhile to adequately show off the item, especially when an item has significant detail. In addition to a front view, a back or side view might be a good idea, as well. Size your photo in such a way that it will load quickly into the browser that your prospective bidder will use. This will, hopefully, keep them viewing your posted item long enough to become interested.

- **Pricing and Duration** You can specify how long you want your listing to run, the number of items available in your grouping of products, and your starting price. Never start the listing price of an item with hopes of getting more. For example, don't hope to get $30 and only start the bidding at $10.

- **Disclose Flaws** Be sure to list thorough descriptions, including dimensions, etc. The more detailed you are, the more likely your buyer is to be satisfied with the purchase. Jeremy says, "Even when there is an apparently small defect, such as a small edge tear on paper items, minor coloration due to aging, or slight damage at the hem of clothing articles, it is always best to disclose them."

- **Disclose All Fees** Be sure you list everything involved in the sale, not only the postage and handling fees but insurance, as well. For example, in the description you may include: "optional insurance for _____ amount," etc. This disclosure will keep your approval ratings high.

- **Layout** Invest the time to strategically place your text and photo(s) when you are selling. This shows the prospective bidder that you are professional. This strategy may require a little education on your part. You may need to learn the simple coding needed to add color, size, and a pleasing font to your text, but this will insure an attractive presentation. You will need to select a title for your item when you list it. This should be a succinct descrip-

Cash for Trash 141

tion (only a few characters are allowed) that uses key words that will attract bidding attention. It is also the key the buyer uses to search.

- **Accepting Payments** You may accept credit card payments through one of the online credit card services offered on eBay by registering. You will need to register a bank account with them for this, so it may be a good idea to set up an account that is exclusively for this. This avoids activity on your family checking account and helps keep things separate.

- **Feedback** Once the transaction is completed, the buyer and seller are allowed to leave a comment on the sale. It will be rated: positive, neutral, or negative. Each positive comment is tallied next to your screen name so that other prospective buyers can see your feedback history. Obviously, this will greatly influence whether someone wants to buy from you again in the future. As a seller, you should always rate the buyer after the transaction is final and you have shipped the item.

- **Customer Service** Deliver your products on time and follow up after the sale to make sure your buyers received their items in good condition. Determine ahead of time what your policy will be if the product is damaged in shipping. Are you going to cover it or say, "Sorry, you didn't buy insurance"?

- **Shipping** Get free boxes and priority-mail packing tape through *www.USPS.com,* and they will also ship them to you free. The catch is that you have to ship the product priority mail, which is generally a good deal if it's over a pound and under five pounds. If the item is over five pounds, it is better to go with UPS ground or FedEx ground.

- **Products That Sell Well** Clothing for 25¢ at a garage sale will sell for $3 on eBay. Some of the bestselling products are brand-name children's clothing and anything that is new and in the original box.
- **"Lot" Sales** If you have ten outfits all the same size, they can be sold in a lot. Picture groupings can be in a lot as well as any group of items that go together—for example, bathroom accessories.

I still have a little space left in this chapter, so I'll leave you with one last important vertical tip:

B
U
Y
*
L
O
W
*
S
E
L
L
*
H
I
G
H

nine

The Pink Slip Blues

Gary Benson, a cousin of our original Benson family (they are a huge dynasty), was a college instructor who taught engineering and truly enjoyed his job. But he made a move to become an aerospace engineer in an often-turbulent industry because his wife, Stella, wanted him to make the big bucks. In fact, she said, "This is the deal, you either quit the college or quit me." So he turned down his "dream" job of a full professorship in order to please his wife. When the company he went with did not get the next huge government contract, he was given sixty days' notice and then was promptly unemployed for eight months. His feelings of insecurity and frustration mounted each day that went by without a job. He felt like a failure, but he also felt resentment toward his wife and her demand that he quit the job he loved. The mind game he routinely played usually ended with "The Blame Game," where he either blamed (1) himself for being weak and not standing up, or (2) his wife.

During the sixty days before he was to be laid off, his wife encouraged him to borrow from everyone they knew to come up with a down payment on a home.

They then purchased a home they would not be able to afford once the layoff took effect. They rationalized that the prospect of making a substantial income within the year when he would be rehired for the next government contract was enough to justify the lean months they were now facing. At least that's what they thought at the time. Gary temporarily took a job as a substitute teacher to pay the bills while he was awaiting callbacks from other aerospace companies. The professorship he'd turned down at the college was no longer available.

But with the big corporate layoff, there were more substitutes than jobs, and Gary found himself at times working only one day a week. It took another eight months for him to find a regular teaching job, and the aerospace company was bought out by another company. But by this time his family was saddled with a huge mortgage based on a ship that never came in. Instead, that ship sank! It would be nice to say that Gary found a better job with a bigger salary and they all lived happily ever after. But that's not what happened.

This couple started to play the "blame game" on a daily basis. Gary dealt with the typical self-esteem issues and guilt that so often accompany someone who is out of work, and he and Stella were pulling in different directions rather than together.

The couple accumulated massive amounts of debt, did not make major modifications to their living standards, and desperately hung on to the dream of greener pastures that would save them from their debt. Sadly, their marriage did not survive the crisis. They divorced and became another statistic. But before you despair, let's look at another Benson cousin and his wife: Richard and Kathryn.

Richard was at the height of his career in retailing.

His store had been selected from among hundreds nationwide as the "Store of the Year" in its field. He was rewarded with a job offer as vice-president in corporate headquarters, which he turned down in order to stay in his current location because he didn't want to move his family. Then he was blindsided by termination. No reason was given for his sudden firing, and he was left to speculate as to *why*.

Richard's vested severance could not be released to him for nearly nine months. So within two months there was suddenly no income but plenty of outgo. Richard said, "I had to learn lessons in trust, waiting, and patience. In trust, I had to ask myself if I really trusted God for His provision. He had provided in the past, but what would my future hold? Then I had to go through the painful character-building experience of waiting. Corporations rarely move quickly with new hires, so patience became another test."

There were times of despair in Richard's life: "I will never forget attending a Fuller Seminary extension class right after being fired. On the first day they went around the room and asked the students to give their names and what they did for a living. I was humiliated beyond belief to say, 'My name is Richard Benson, and I'm unemployed.' I thought I would die. I have since learned to say, 'I am unencumbered by employment.' "

Richard was willing to start over in a new career (after a decade in his old one) and began working part time in the area of freelance editing. He borrowed money from a family member at no interest to buy a computer to accommodate his new job, and he sold advertising part time to supplement his income as he built expertise in his new profession. A decade later he is again at the top of his field, having obtained an industry-wide award for his expertise, which was very similar to the award he won in retail. He loves his new job and realizes that he wouldn't have had such an opportunity if he hadn't been fired.

Still, it wasn't a bed of roses. Richard says, "Some people have said that being fired worked out for the best. That may be true, but it doesn't make getting fired 'right.' It was a decision not based on facts or with any ethical basis. We suffered financially for nearly ten years because of it. I still harbor a seed of resentment for that trauma to our family's future. While we feel somewhat secure now, I would say that if I had zero income and no opportunities, we couldn't last more than three months at our current standard of living. That is how little we were able to save. We've only been able to truly save for the past three years."

One of the things that made the biggest difference, according to Richard, was his wife's response to the crisis. He says,

> She was extremely supportive of me. Sure she cried, very hard, when I came home with the news. But she watched carefully as I went through all the various stages of the experience. She never doubted me or that God would take care of us. (I did all the worrying and doubting—enough for both of us!) She controls the daily household expenses, so she was the one who made the household cutbacks. She also explained the situation to our kids and helped them understand what Daddy was going through. Our children were ten, seven, and four at the time. One simple cost-saving thing we did was use paper bags the grocery store provides versus buying plastic garbage bags. Eight years later, when my present employer made me a full-time employee, I bought

a box of plastic garbage bags—it was a symbolic thing for me. We still use the paper ones, it is a simple savings, but for me it remains a constant reminder of harder times.

When I was convinced that I needed to buy a computer and to begin working from home, Kathryn was supportive despite her serious dislike of technology and anything associated with it. She still says she is a card-carrying member of the Lead Pencil Club. In later years she bought me a huge desk and a sort of antique credenza that I use every day. Before, I was working off a very old student desk with one small drawer. I still marvel at how she handled the whole situation. I never felt nagged or pushed into something I didn't want to do. I talked to her every day about each and every call and inquiry big or small. We discussed the whole issue of moving at length. It was a mutually agreed upon spiritual decision to stay. Not to say that we didn't have our problems, because we had plenty. But Kathryn supported me throughout the whole ordeal.

Two Families, Choices, and Outcomes

Even though the two Benson families are kissin' cousins, they are worlds apart when it comes to how they handled unemployment. Consequently, there were vastly different outcomes for their families. Gary chose to leave his job, hoping for something better, but never really had a good feeling about that decision before he made it. Both were later out of work, for uncertain and seemingly unjust reasons, and both certainly wondered *why?* But Gary and Stella got caught up in the blame game and it led to divorce court. Richard and Kathryn pulled together, and it led to hard-earned financial and marital stability.

Gary and Stella bought a house based on an uncertain future—he didn't have the high-paying job they were hoping for, and he was about to take an indefinite vacation from work. Rather than make dramatic cutbacks, Gary and Stella maintained their standard of living and put everything on a credit card, and when their credit limit was maxed out they borrowed *to make a down payment* on a house they couldn't afford. Richard borrowed only enough money to buy a computer—a tool that would contribute to making an income. Gary and Stella had a superficial faith, but it didn't come through in a pinch. Richard and Kathryn had a solid faith that saw them through the tough times.

These are true stories that happened to real people (names and occupations have been changed). How *you* survive a season of unemployment will depend upon (1) the sacrifices you are willing to make, (2) your attitude, and (3) your faith. Let's look at six ways to make it through when you're out of a job—and feeling out on a limb.

The Six "S" Words for Those "Unencumbered by Employment"

There are six main things to keep in mind when you are searching for a job: success, spending, saving, searching, a sense of humor, and sanctuary.

Success

Readjust Your Expectations in All Areas

When times are lean, it's a great occasion to readjust

all aspects of your family's life. Redefine success—it's not necessarily found in your lifestyle. For example, redefine your definition of entertainment—it doesn't have to be expensive. Rediscover the challenge of board games, enjoy the beauty of a walk in a park, or check out a new hiking trail. Instead of going out for dinner and a movie, choose one outing per week—either/or. Consider going to a matinee or a dollar theater and eat at home. Or, review the "Lifestyles" section of your local paper and eat at a restaurant that offers midweek dining specials. Check the FSIs (free standing inserts) in your Sunday paper for restaurant coupons.

There will need to be readjustments in where your family shops for clothing and especially how much you are willing to pay. If your children are in a private school, they may need to go public or homeschool for a year or two. You may need to temporarily become a one-car family or trade down your second car to acquire some much-needed cash. Unemployment is a radical time in a family's life, and it demands radical changes in order to survive without accruing a debt load that could take years to pay off.

Encourage in Tangible Ways

Let's look at another couple who found a good path to travel in their unemployment journey: Stephanie and Michael. People who have been laid off may feel like a failure when they cannot provide for their family, which can lead to a cycle of depression and lethargy. Stephanie faced this problem when her husband's telecommunications corporation downsized and eliminated his job. Michael sent out résumés, followed up on leads, and was still out of work for many months. The mounting tension left both partners feeling defeated.

Under the advice of their pastor, Stephanie urged Michael to set up a budget for the little money they had coming in. They also looked for active ways to save money and be grateful for God's provision, however that might be manifested. Stephanie practiced mock job interviews with Michael and helped him work on his résumé to make it more marketable for the specific firms that he applied to.

In Stephanie's situation, she made a choice that she would praise every positive step Michael took. Soon her speech shifted from placating platitudes to genuine gratefulness. Instead of saying, "Cheer up, you'll find work soon," she said, "Thanks for getting such a bargain on those cleats at the thrift store; Junior will love them." Michael became a near-expert in saving money at the grocery store and actually cut their food budget in half after he bought my book *Shop, Save, and Share*. By saving in practical ways and encouraging each other, this couple weathered the storm until Michael was once again gainfully employed full time. Their marriage was strengthened, they had greater compassion for those in financial need, and they never forgot that contentment is a choice.

Spending

Clothing Options

Being content is often a choice. Redefine what "needed clothing" really is. Some families who used to let their kids wear certain brands are suddenly shopping at discount department stores when they become unemployed. Learn to update your family's wardrobe with a selection from a local consignment store. These choices can save as much as 40 percent on your clothing budget, and some of the items are still new with the original tags present. For example, my friend Heather is a professional woman who wears suits to work daily. When her husband was laid off of his job, she was the sole breadwinner—and she certainly needed an up-to-date wardrobe! Her job as a television producer required a trendy look, and yet she said, "I now get most of my clothes at an upscale consignment store downtown. I paid half price for a Perry Ellis wool coat that looks fabulous over my suits."

If you have kids, trade off some of your children's clothing with another family who has kids in corresponding sizes. For example, the Brazell family has a seven-year-old boy and a nine-year-old girl. They trade their outgrown clothing with the Taylor family, who has a six-year-old boy and a ten-year-old girl.

Get Your Kids to Pitch In!

When the Hollibaugh family faced yet another non-renewal of a construction contract and found the dad out of a job, the kids pitched in! It reminded me of an episode of the timeless series *Little House on the Prairie*. Charles Ingalls had an accident and couldn't work to meet his loan note. He was set to forfeit the oxen necessary for their livelihood. Instead, Ma went to work in the fields, baby Carrie hauled potatoes, Mary sewed for Mrs. Whipple, and Laura did Mary's chores and brought home her schoolwork. At the end of the episode, the family had earned enough money to pay the note and keep the oxen. Upon seeing the love and determination of the Ingalls family, the wealthy town merchant, Mr. Oleson, told Charles, "I do believe you're the wealthiest man in town."

By explaining their financial situation to their kids,

ages fifteen, thirteen, eleven, and nine, Mom and Dad Hollibaugh enlisted their help in weathering this difficult season. The children became expert shoppers at garage sales and helped their family save tons on quality household goods and clothing. For example, Brandon found blue jeans for $5 that were normally $50 in the store. Whitney found three beautiful Laura Ashley dresses for only $6 each. Ryan found two bikes for $25 at a garage sale. He used one bike for parts and the other became his younger brother's birthday present.

Your kids may not necessarily go out and get jobs, but their contribution can be as simple as not complaining about the lack of expensive snack foods or pricey entertainment and learning how to be thrifty shoppers.

Keep Paying Down Debt

Even when we are unemployed (or underemployed), we sometimes receive unexpected sources of income—temporary work, an insurance premium refund, or a generous birthday check from extended family. If these additional monies are not needed for basic household expenses, immediately apply them toward debt reduction.

By continuing to pay down debt, you avoid additional interest and thereby "earn" that extra amount each month you pay off your debts early. When our family was $40,000 in debt and Bob took a $15,000 a year pay cut to go into the Air Force, we purposed to become good financial stewards. Instead of vacations that added up to big bucks, we took several day trips to free parks and recreation centers. We went out to eat only once every two weeks, which became a special treat during that time. The main thing we did was continue to pay our tithe first, and it was amazing how everything else fell into place. Within three years we were debt free. It can be done. There is hope.

Saving

A Penny Saved Is More Than a Penny Earned

Once you readjust your expectations and focus on staying content, start cutting back in practical ways. A penny saved is more than a penny earned because you don't have to pay interest or taxes on "saved" pennies. Let's say you want to add $200 per month to your current budget. To achieve your goal, you simply *stop spending* the $200 per month and pocket it. Conversely, if you wanted to add $200 per month to your budget by *earning* it, you would actually have to make $260+ per month to cover taxes and social security. If the average family cuts their food budget by 30 percent, they would save around $2,400 per year, or $200 per month. A family member would have to earn $3,100 on the economy to make the equivalent. So every time you save money, you earn money.

When my friend Kelli, a single mom with three boys, got laid off from one of her two part-time jobs, she worried about making ends meet. She was able to follow the above example of saving on her food bill, and the results were incredible. Her boys helped her clip coupons, organize the shopping trip, and find sales at the store. She found that the extra income from the second job was made up in grocery savings. She was able to drop the job and spend more time at home with her children.

When the breadwinner is out of work, they feel the additional burden of "not doing anything" to contribute financially. But cutting back *is* an active contribution to the household budget and will make the money go further until another job comes through.

A penny saved is more than a penny earned because you don't have to pay interest or taxes on "saved" pennies.

Insurance Savings

One of the most painless ways to save is to examine your insurance coverage. Michael said, "I changed our homeowner's policy to cover only catastrophic losses. This increased deductible and more limited coverage decreased our payments by $50 a month. When I was gainfully employed again, we reverted back to our original policy limitations."

If you don't already have higher deductibles on the comprehensive and collision portion of your auto policy, then request that change for a potential savings of hundreds of dollars per year. Ask your agent for all the discounts you may qualify for, including non-smokers' policy, driver's education courses, an alarm on your car, or credits for a good driving record. When one of my readers, Sally, called for her discounts, she discovered that she was still on a policy for high-risk drivers from an accident that had been off her record for seven years. She wrote, "Since I had no moving violations in the last three years, I was moved up to a policy reserved for good drivers and now I'm saving 50 percent on my automobile insurance!"

Health insurance is usually a big issue for people who were formerly covered on their employer's policy.

The COBRA (*www.cobrahealth.com*) option allows you to stay covered under your former employer's group policy, but you pay the premiums instead of your employer. You might want to look into a policy that many people in full-time ministry choose—The Golden Rule Insurance Company at *www.goldenrule.com*. Michael said, "We chose the $5,000 deductible option, basically covering catastrophic losses. We paid for all our doctor's visits and prescriptions, and then we prayed for good health."

Barter or Defer Payments to Keep Continuity

Stephanie negotiated with her daughters' piano and dance teachers to continue lessons and then pay when Michael was employed again—which they did, in one lump sum. "Keeping continuity was important for our kids," says Stephanie. "They needed that sense of stability, and their teachers were willing to help us in this way. If we had canceled the lessons, without asking, our children would have lost out."

Or, you could provide goods or services in exchange for lessons. One family I know exchanged housework for piano lessons for a few months while their dad was out of work (with the kids helping out on the housework, too). Another option would be to put the proceeds of a family garage sale toward these specific areas.

Searching

Job Search and Interview Strategies

Do one thing each day in your job search—no matter how small. Make a call, send an e-mail, mail a letter, update a résumé, or search on a job Web site. Be diligent about this, because your new job has just become "finding a job." You aren't paid for this work, but you will get paid when you find work.

While you're cutting costs in all areas by temporarily suspending cable TV and multiple cell phones, and you've converted all your long-distance service to a pre-paid card that costs 3.5 cents per minute (Sam's, Costco), you do not want to cut off Internet service or your daily newspaper. The paper provides lists of information and job openings, and the Internet can be a great source for the same. Realize that every lead will not turn into a great job. Accept each nibble with excitement, but balance it with wisdom and discernment. Check out *www.monster.com* to find résumé help, industry data, and salary data.

While you're searching, ask yourself, "Will this job be good for me in three years?" Spouses who want to help their unemployed partners should be aware of the fact that depression and despair can settle into someone who has been searching many months for work. Instead of asking, "So who did you talk to about getting a job?" simply ask, "How was your day?" Don't forget to verbally encourage your spouse as we saw in the previous example in this chapter. You might also give an uplifting book, such as *Devotions for Job Seekers* by Richard Malone (Doubleday/Galilee, 2003), which provides encouraging daily reading for you or your spouse.

Consider getting "cross employment" temporarily while in employment transition. This is where you are trained to do a different kind of work until you can find a permanent situation. A friend of mine was trained by H&R Block to get certified as a tax accountant to create some part-time income and keep busy in a workplace while she searched for a permanent position. It still remains a fallback position during uncertain economic seasons. File for unemployment if you haven't already; it is a justifiable, temporary source of income for this transition period.

Interview Quick Tips

- **Practice Makes Perfect** If you or someone in your family is interviewing for a job, conduct mock interviews at home. Try to think of questions that are likely to be asked. This can make the difference between a comfortable interview and an unsuccessful one.

- **Know the Type of Interview in Advance** The basic types of interviews are: traditional, behavioral, video-conferencing, panel, or telephone interview. By knowing the type of process involved, the practice sessions will be more targeted toward the actual interview.

- **Be Prepared** Articulate what makes you (or your spouse) stand out from other candidates—identify strengths, skills, and accomplishments. In the résumé, organize qualifications by category to provide an easy read for the interviewer. Research the organization. Gather as much data about the position as possible and attend any information sessions offered by the company.

- **Nonverbal Communication** Practice positive nonverbal behaviors, such as a pleasant tone of voice, good eye contact, relaxed hands, nodding in response, and leaning your body toward the interviewer. During the mock interview, the "interviewer" should make note of negative nonverbal responses, such as poor eye contact, yawning, closing the eyes, too rapid or too slow a rate of speech, arms folded tightly, chewing gum, or distracting gestures.

- **Clothing Guidelines** Know the job attire and dress accordingly. Simple clothing should be worn that is cleaned, pressed, and appropriate to the profession. Use moderate cologne and makeup (for women). Limit the amount of jewelry you wear, and arrive early to find a mirror and check the status of your appearance.

- **During the Interview, Don't Say:** "I'm so worried about 'blowing' this interview." "Do you know any good unemployment strategies?" "What kind of person doesn't get the job?" or anything negative about your previous employer(s).

A Sense of Humor

The high value placed on humor should be evident throughout this book. When you laugh, not only are endorphins released (a natural stimulant), but you'll have less chance for ulcers and other health problems, as well. I'm amazed at how I can laugh at driving through two garage doors in a year or surviving the births of five babies in seven years, but I can! Take time to recount the funny stories in your family. Watch old family videotapes or look through the photo album. It will remind you of times when it was a little easier to laugh and will help you put your present and future into perspective. Rent (or check out from the library) a favorite comedy film or joke book. Have a stand-up comedy night at home with your family. Visit with a friend who makes you laugh, and steer clear of naysayers.

Sanctuary

Unusual circumstances sometimes call for special help. We all need a sanctuary from the cares of life. Find a trusted friend to vent with when you are frustrated with your search or with your spouse. We seek advice for our finances, in parenting issues, and in marriage situations—why should it be different to get some counsel during a job transition? Seek out free job counseling from nonprofit organizations such as the Small Business Development Center (*www.sba.gov*) and see what courses and counseling they offer that will help you in your employment pursuits.

In Richard and Gary's cases, both were without a job quite suddenly. This led to a variety of emotions similar to the grief process: shock, denial, depression, anger, and acceptance. Sometimes people need to work through these feelings with a counselor either alone or with a spouse. Go to a trusted nonprofit counselor at your church or community health center to help work through these issues. If you do not have a good sense of where to go for this kind of assistance in your community, go to the American Association of Christian Counselors at *www.aacc.net*.

Finally, if you haven't developed a quality prayer life, you have time to do it now! There is one sanctuary that will never let you down and where you can truly find peace. Let God know the details of your day, your fears and frustrations as well as your joys and sorrows. He's always home and His line is never busy.

❧ ten ❧

The Seventh-Day Rest
When Penny-Pinching Gets Old

Today was a perfect day. The kids woke up in a good mood and helped one another get ready for school. Daniel offered to make all the lunches, and Bob suggested he drive the kids to school so I could get out the door for an early walk around the neighborhood. I came home to a fabulous bubble bath in our whirlpool tub and read a chapter from the latest book in the *Mitford* series. Then I went to Starbucks and had a Venti Decaf Mocha with my best girl friend. My editor called on my cell phone and said that I'd worked so hard on this deadline that the publishers were going to pay for my girl friend and me to take a shopping trip to Hawaii—today. I called Bob and said I'd be a bit late because I had to go pick up a few things in Hawaii, and could he pick up the kids from school? Bob told me to spend a few extra days there and not to worry about the kids.

I lay on the beach in my swimsuit, which was too big because I'd miraculously lost twenty pounds overnight after a trip to the luxury hotel's "body wrap therapy" room. When life got too strenuous on the beach, I walked ten feet to the massage therapists' hut, and they gave me a two-hour massage. I left there feeling so relaxed and thin and beautiful that I was stopped on the beach by a famous Hollywood producer who asked me to be the next "Bond girl." I promptly turned him down because of the morality clause in my publishing contract.

Then I saw my arch nemesis, Dave Meurer, who is the witty author of *The Hair-Raising Joys of Raising Boys* and a merciless practical joker who hounds me when I'm on deadline. His appearance on the beach was about to spoil my perfectly good day, until he told me that the publisher made him pay his *own* way to Hawaii. And he had to travel by cattle barge (and I didn't even know they had cattle barges going to the islands)! And once he got there, his flowered lei made him break out in hives and he fainted on the beach and no one noticed because he looks like the living dead even when he's alive. He was unconscious for six hours in the sun and got as red as a lobster and now his cattle barge was leaving and he had to go back home after never getting to enjoy this tropical paradise.

Yes, it was a perfect day in every way.

Sigh.

And then I woke up.

I'd overslept and would have to rush to get the kids out the door and the lunches made and the deadline met. We still don't have a Starbucks in our small town. We have only a Super Wal-Mart that serves a five-cent cup of coffee to senior citizens. My kids are in the height of sibling rivalry and don't know what "talk quietly" even means—much less how to do it. My husband is gone on a military trip and my publishing house is being sold and my editor is sending me nasty messages in the form of a desk plaque that reads: "If deadlines weren't threatening, they wouldn't begin with *dead*."

My best girl friends all live out of state, and Hawaii is just a picture on a postcard that my "dear" friend sent after she lost thirty pounds and went there to celebrate. A swimsuit is not my friend, and Dave Meurer is still bothering me like a bad bowl of chili.

Sigh.

But it's fun to dream, isn't it?

———

Sometimes pinching pennies can get old.

Real old.

Way old.

Big time old.

Stinkin' old.

Big, fat, double-dog-ugly old.

That's why it's important to take time off and build in rest. I know that when I schedule time off from deadlines to rest, I'm a happier person (my family can attest to this). When I work hard, I treat myself to something special. And that keeps me healthy and productive and gives me something to look forward to.

When God created the world in six days, He took the seventh day off as a day to rest. And if God did it, then we can do it, too. In fact, if God rested, then by *not* resting I might somehow imply that I'm better than God, right?

So you need to overcome frugal burnout by living *well* while living within your means. Here are some (sad and even bizarre, but true) signs of frugal burnout:

- You ask your grandmother to start saving foil in little balls for you.
- You are at the pizza shop, and the couple next to

you leaves half a pizza untouched and uneaten, and you ask the waitress for a carryout box.

- You live in California and pull over your Mercedes Wannabe to pick up an orange you see lying by the side of the road.
- To save water—you keep your fish in the toilet bowl and train it to cling to the sides at the first sound of rushing water.
- You search the Internet for creative ways to use those bits of soap that are too little to use but too big to throw away.
- You overhear your seven-year-old son say that one day he wants to make *so much* money that he can "go to the movies even when it's not *dollar night.*"
- You resent the fact that everyone else is out spending, while you're counting pennies from a Mason jar.
- You won't go to Blockbuster on Thursday through Sunday because on Monday through Wednesday you can get the "rent one/get one free" videos with your "rewards" membership.
- You find yourself trying to figure out ways to recycle the cotton balls you take from the top of your vitamin bottle.
- When your friend asks you to meet her for lunch, you try to talk her into a restaurant she doesn't like because it offers a "buy one/get one free" and you can get the free lunch.
- You wear the same clothes three days in a row in order to "get your money's worth" out of the wash.
- You wash and reuse plastic Ziploc bags.

Yep, if you find yourself doing any of these things you are well on your way to frugal burnout. And yet you wouldn't believe how many times people think that I teach others to save by doing some of the things on this list.

No! No! No!

You don't have to live like an obsessive Scrooge in order to save money! Pay down your debts and live within your means. You can live well and have fun, and I aim to show you how. Here are a few ways to help you come up with your own way of celebrating the "Seventh-Day Rest." Choose one or more, put it on your calendar, and start celebrating.

You don't have to live like an obsessive Scrooge in order to save money! Pay down your debts and live within your means.

Reminders

You have to remind yourself why you're saving. Is it for personal financial freedom? To get out of debt? To save for a house? To put your kids through college? To retire early? To go on a special vacation? Write down the "whys" of your frugal living plan and post it where you can review it regularly. Better yet, get a tangible reminder of your goal—something that will make you feel good about being diligent financially. Here are some ideas:

- **Chart** One woman plotted her debts on a chart so

she could measure how quickly she was paying off her credit card debt. She watched her balance go down as her spirit soared.

- **Cards** Another woman printed a card to carry in her wallet that read, "Debt Free, That's for Me!" Every time she took money out, she saw her card and was reminded of her goals.

- **Trips** If you want to own a dream home one day, take a free drive to some of the houses in the country or in that neighborhood where you'd like to live. What a great reminder of where you would like to be one day.

- **Pat on the Back** Every time you make it through a month better than you did the month before, take time to pat yourself on the back. Sometimes these "pats" can be more tangible than just a physical tap. But more on that in the next section.

Support Systems

If you have a goal in mind, you need to see what places or people cause that goal to get short-circuited. If going to Neiman Marcus sets off your "dissatisfaction signals," then stay away from there. If you have a friend who derides you for being thrifty, loves to show you her newest outfit and latest ring, or talks about the new custom SUV she's ordered, then find a frugal friend instead. Here are a few options:

- **Internet** Check out some of the Internet sites and message boards devoted to frugal living by doing a *google.com* search on the topic. There are new ones springing up all the time.

- **Coupon Clubs** Form your own "coupon club" as I discuss in *How to Save Money Every Day*. People in these clubs swap coupons using a coupon swap box and have fun sharing the different coupon values in your area.

- **E-mail Clubs** This requires a central person who receives daily submissions from frugal spies who see a special clearance, unadvertised value, or other discounts in your locality. The central person sends out a daily (or weekly) e-mail alert on what you can get free with coupons or other values. This helps you have fun with new friends while saving.

Carpe Diem

There's nothing like "seizing the day" to make you feel rested and refreshed. Focusing on what you don't have is a setup for discontentment, but focusing on what you have sets you up for taking pleasure in the simple things.

- **Home, Sweet Home** Rather than being bothered by the fact that you don't have your dream home, you can make your current home more cozy, clean, and comfy. Paint is cheap and so is fabric. Paint some of your furniture and cover a lampshade or even an entire wall in fabric. Check out some of the frugal decorating tips from *My Name Isn't Martha, But I Can Decorate My Home* by Sharon Hanby Robie (Pocket Books, 1998).

- **Journals** Keep a list of all the things you are grateful for and all the ways your life has improved since embarking on your savings journal. Some of your family members could be the first entries on a list like that. Include other things you may take for granted, such as your health, cultural surroundings, or beautiful aspects of your climate and area.

- **Speak It** Negative and positive self-talk do make a difference. If you tell yourself that you hate your life enough, you will start to believe it. On the other hand, if you say things like "Everything I love most is right here within these walls," then you'll believe *that*, too. Every time you are hounded by a demon of negativism that whispers things like "You'll never be out of debt" or "You never have any fun," discipline yourself to automatically replace that thought with "I'm going to be debt free one day" or "I find a lot of fun in the funny things my kids do each day!"

- **Family and Friends** People who find satisfaction in frugal living also have the benefit of spending quality time with friends and family. They are not constantly on the go with expensive distractions but can find a tremendous amount of fun and satisfaction in playing games with friends or being challenged with lively discussions.

- **Theme Nights** Create a biweekly night of fun with your family and structure it around a theme, depending upon the ages of your children. You could have "movie" nights with "buy one/get one free" rentals, popcorn, and homemade cookies. Young children will love a stay-up-till-your-eyelids-fall-off night (even though they may not be able to keep themselves awake past ten). Mexican fiesta night features special foods, Latin music, and your family practicing their best Spanish accents (I have mine down pat, since my mom was born in Spain).

The Seventh-Day Splurge

Okay, here's the fun part—a built-in, no-kidding, honest-to-goodness *splurge*. Every budget, even the tightest, needs a little wiggle room to enjoy "fun money." You put it into your budget at the top level, remember? Create a specific way to wisely spend this, rather than wasting it on a series of little things. You can make spending this money mandatory, if you'd like.

Use some of the tips I've listed to save money in the area of entertainment and plan that night out for dinner, a trip to the zoo, movie night, or a visit to the amusement park. Save for a special, fabulous, yet affordable vacation that your family will remember forever. Put it on your calendar, calculate how much you need to save each week, and look forward to both long-term and short-term splurges.

Another idea is to commit smaller amounts of "found" money, such as rebates and coupon savings, to pay for movie and dinner dates. Sure, the larger windfall checks should go to reducing consumer debt, but it's perfectly all right to "splurge" with these special treats. A night out can help in many ways by allowing you to connect with family members, by helping you to unwind, and by reinforcing the fact that you can stay on a budget and still have a blast.

Some other ideas include splurging on a weekly bouquet of flowers for your home, setting aside a special afternoon to buy ice-cream cones, changing your regular routine, or exploring your own city.

A Fool Has No Peace

I know you've heard the old saying "A fool and his money are soon parted." And this paragraph centers in on non-fools. Wisdom is knowing how and when to spend money. Ultimately, you will be able to rest better when you are at peace about your financial goals and the vehicle you've chosen to get there. The next time you're tempted to be discontented because your neighbor has a new car or a bigger house or is going on a fancy vacation, think some basic facts through carefully. One CPA said that he "has clients who have incomes of two to three times that of other clients, but have less equity in their homes and property because of their tremendous debt loads" (Liz Pulliam Weston, *www.moneycentral.msn.com,* 2002). Your neighbor might just have a ton of debt and is spending money foolishly.

You don't have the debt load of someone who spends money foolishly, or if you do, you're getting rid of yours. If the average consumer has $8,000 worth of debt and you have $7,999, you have less than average! Many of the people of whom you are envious have tremendous debt problems or find their satisfaction in "things." These "fools" may carelessly pay too much for the very same item for which you paid a dime on the dollar. Fools are out of control in their spending, but non-fools are in charge of their outgo.

Four Axioms of Spending

There are four basic axioms of spending, as Howard L. Dayton Jr. writes in *Getting Out of Debt Pocket Guide* (Tyndale House, 1986):

1. *The more shopping we do, the more we spend.*
2. *The more we watch television, the more we spend.*
3. *The more time we spend looking through catalogs, the more we spend.*
4. *The more we read magazines and newspaper advertisements, the more we spend.*

These are all pastimes that can lead to frugal burnout because they tempt you to be discontent with your life and go out and do something about it—like spend money! Consequently, I think we need four axioms to keep us from frugal burnout:

1. Shop *less* and you will save *more*.
2. Watch *less* television and save *more*.
3. *Throw away* mail order catalogs and save *more*.
4. *Bypass* reading the advertisements in magazines and newspapers and save *more*.

In conclusion, this chapter is more about attitude than action. You can avoid frugal burnout with wise choices. It's about choosing to pursue rest with all your strength and being content on your financial journey to making your dreams come true.

Now, if you'll excuse me, I think I'll go take a nap.

eleven

Room by Room Savings

Saving on the Essentials

I'm a drama queen.

Always have been.

Always will be.

It runs in the family.

Recently six out of seven of us were in a local adaptation of *The Christmas Carol*. Bob was Ebenezer Scrooge, Philip was a merchant, Bethany was young Belle (Ebenezer's youthful girlfriend), Jonathan was Tiny Tim, Joshua was an unruly student (he's being typecast), and I was Mrs. Cobbler, a thieving Cockney maid (no offense to Cockneys).

I was loud, conniving, and had sticky fingers. Totally out of character for me. But I'm the drama queen, so I made do. During the dinner theater production, the caterer needed more time to prepare the prime rib, so the producer asked me to go out and "warm up the crowd," (which was ravenous and waiting for meat, mind you).

I went up to the first table and shouted, "'ello! 'ow are ye doin'?"

Everyone just stared, their faces as cold as stone. This was going to be a tough crowd, one even Rodney Dangerfield would have trouble with. So I pulled out my secret weapon—"the diva theme."

Imagining myself as Eliza Doolittle from *My Fair Lady*, I said, "I'm a gud gurl, I am! I washed me face an' 'ands before I come!"

A few of the ice statues started to melt, and I saw a smile here and there, which only encouraged me, I'm afraid.

"You know, I'm a star of this hee-yah pro-duc-tion! I've axed fo' me own trailer, personal assistant, and a team of backup dan-cers!" The audience started to laugh—loudly.

Just as I was on a roll, I got pulled backstage because the prime rib was done and, well, so was I. Bob was a fabulous Scrooge with a great British accent. In my big scene, a laundress, a charwoman, and a pawnbroker were called "birds of a feather." We (allegedly) stole Scrooge's silver after he was dead—but they couldn't pin anything on me! In the scene, I put a pewter mug in my purse that I'd stolen, and then I was to take it out again before the final scene of the play.

Only I forgot to take it out.

After Scrooge has his conversion experience, he raises my wages from two shillings a week to ten shillings, and I scream and twirl around in a circle as my (allegedly empty) purse is supposed to accidentally hit Scrooge in the face.

Except the purse had the large pewter mug in it, and everyone in the audience heard it clang loudly against Scrooge's face!

Then, in response to his out-of-character generosity,

I ask, "Mistah Scrooge, you want that I should call for the doctor?"

Bob was supposed to say, "No. Not the doctor nor the undertaker . . ."

But as he stood rubbing his sore chin, he said, "Why, I think I'd like a doctor!"

———

It just goes to show you that even when life is scripted, it doesn't always go according to plan. But even when an unexpected financial setback derails our dreams—we always have another chance. This chapter is chock-full of dozens of ways you can continue to cut back and get back on track. To make it easier, I've divided the savings ideas into the various rooms of your house.

A great proverb says, "By wisdom a house is built, and through understanding it is established; through knowledge its rooms are filled with rare and beautiful treasures" (Proverbs 24:3). When Bob and I first married, we had a cross-stitch plaque on our wall that read: "Blessed are the poor, for they be us." I remember how we prayed our way through each room in our house, asking God for the items we needed but couldn't afford. Step by step, saving in little ways not only got us out of debt, but it helped us make ends meet during a very difficult financial season of life. But the most amazing aspect of saving in little ways was how much better we were able to sleep at night. We could rest easy knowing that we were doing the right things to get out of debt. We were resting in the fact that we were no longer lost without a road map, but we were on our way toward freedom.

We've come a long way since our modest beginnings

but still love the thrill of saving money and being good stewards of our resources. If you need to cut costs in a simple, unencumbered way, here are some easy ways to look around your house and experience the "rest" of saving money room by room:

Family Room

- *Coverings.* If you have young children at home, you may want to wait to have your furniture recovered. By purchasing a quality slipcover for $65 instead of buying a new sofa for $850, you save $785. By placing a crocheted doily for $15 on the coffee table to cover scratches made by a speeding Corvette (Hot Wheels size), you save $115 over buying a new table for $130.
- *Quick cleaning.* Spills on carpeting and furniture are best attacked as soon as they happen. It's a wise idea to keep carpet and upholstery cleaner nearby, and be sure your baby-sitter knows how to use it, too. If the carpet must be professionally cleaned, it will cost about $95 more than using a $10 can of spot cleaner.
- *Subscriptions.* Magazines that are taking up space could possibly be consolidated or even canceled. Consider sharing a subscription with a friend or relative; the average American subscribes to two to three magazines that they never read. This can save up to $90 per year.

Garage

- *Gas mileage.* Take out the excess weight in your trunk and have your tire pressure checked on a regular basis to save approximately 5¢ a gallon in better gas mileage. This saves about $75 per year per car. You can also go to *www.gaspricewatch.com* to help you find the lowest prices at the pump for some 127,000 gas stations.

- *Insurance for young drivers.* Put your old jalopy in your child's name and make him the principle driver on a vehicle that does not carry full coverage. This could save $400 on a premium that might run as much as $1,400 per year.
- *Cars.* The cheapest car to drive is the paid-for one you now own—even if some repairs are needed! Taking care of the car you have, with regular maintenance and oil changes, is more cost effective than buying a new one. But if you need another car, first research the current list of the most reliable *used* cars according to automotive researcher J. D. Power and Associates at *www.jdpower.com*.

Bathrooms

- *Saving water.* Don't put bricks in your toilet tanks to displace water—they could decompose and clog up your pipes. Instead, use a water-filled quart plastic container that will not interfere with the plunger and save as much as $100 per year.
- *Linens.* Buy the same color towels and linens to save big bucks every year. For example, if you choose all white towels, you won't have to buy a new set if one is stained or mildewed. The same goes for sheets— choose all white, and you will only have to buy a top sheet or a fitted sheet if they are torn or damaged. This can save $45 a year on towels and $65 a year on sheets.

- *Repair now, save later.* Broken tiles and chipped grout in the bathroom should be fixed immediately in order to minimize water damage to tiles and the wallboard. Water damage costs an average of $300 compared to a simple $30 tile repair—save $270.

Baby's Room

- *Baby shower.* If you are expecting, and haven't had a baby shower yet, take inventory of what you really need for your baby—including the sizes of clothing you still need. When the hostess asks you for a list of items you'd like, be sure to include larger sizes in appropriate seasons. I outfitted our daughter for the first two years of her life by doing this, for a total savings of $700!
- *Baby stuff.* Babies outgrow clothing—as well as toys and other paraphernalia—so quickly that it rarely pays to pay full price. Borrow or swap with another mom or pick up quality, unstained clothing, bedding, toys, and more at garage sales and used clothing stores.
- *Baby wipes.* Consider making your own to save $100 per year per baby. I did this for all five of our children until they were well into their toddler years. Just take a two-ply high quality roll of paper towels and cut the roll in half (I use a large serrated bread knife). Then purchase a ten-cup plastic bowl with a snap-on lid. Cut an X in the middle of the lid. Place one-half cup of baby wash, one-half cup of baby shampoo, and one-half cup of baby oil into the bowl and mix well. Add one cup of water, place the half roll of paper towels into the mixture, and allow it to absorb for two minutes, then turn it over

(with the cut side down) and allow the rest of the liquid to be absorbed into the towels. If they are not wet through, then add water in one-fourth-cup increments until you get the amount that matches your humidity factors and towel absorbency. Once the center cardboard is wet, remove it and thread the towels, from the center of the roll, through the *X* in the lid.

Kitchen

- *Combine oven dishes.* Select menu items that will cook at the same temperature rather than heating the oven twice at two different times. This could save $95 in annual energy costs.
- *Cloth napkins and real plates.* It's cheaper to wash than to buy paper—although it's less convenient. This tip can save almost $75 per year.
- *Check seals* on your refrigerator and clean the coils to save $30 per year on energy costs.

Kitchen Bonus: Slashing the Food Budget (a mini *Shop, Save, and Share* course)

- **Just Say "No"—Look "High and Low" for Bargains**

    Marketing experts depend on impulse buying. They place the most expensive items at eye level and the bargains on the upper and lower shelves. Look high and low for the best deals—and say no to the pricey stuff.
- **Shop to Share—Be a Provision for Others in Need**

When you combine coupons and store sales to get an item for pennies or *free*—then you're in a position to share these goods with a local food pantry or a family in need. You become God's provision for others.

- **Be Tax Savvy—Get a Deduction for Sharing**

  When you donate groceries to a nonprofit organization (or the church), ask for a receipt. Keep your grocery receipts and highlight the donated item. Current tax laws allow you to deduct the value of the item as a donation (the price *before* coupons since coupons are considered *cash tendered*). You'll need to itemize, and I recommend you check with a tax specialist each year to keep up-to-date on this deduction.

- **Shop Alone—Leave the Little Ones at Home**

  If possible—leave the babies at home or with a friend. Sans kids, concentration is much better and you're less likely to make quick, costly decisions.

- **Don't Leave Home Without It!—Take Your List**

  It's a known fact among consumer researchers that people who shop with a list (and stick to it) consistently spend as much as 30 percent less. Using a list will not only save you money, it will save you time, too.

- **Don't Fight the Crowds**

  The least busy times at the store are Thursday evenings and Saturday mornings. Without the pressure of a crowded store, you'll spend less *and* stress less.

- **Shop the Loss Leaders**

  A loss leader is an advertised item designed to entice buyers into a store. Often the store will lose money on these products, but they'll make up the difference when Aunt Harriet comes to their store for her weekly shopping. If you have the time, shop the loss leaders at each store and leave the regular-priced stuff for dear Auntie.

- **Clip Coupons**

    Yes, clipping coupons really works. Do you think it's not worth your time? My average grocery receipt is $120 before coupons and only $50 (or less) after coupons. (For more help on doing the same, read *Shop, Save, and Share*.)

- **Double Your Savings**

    I prefer shopping at a store that offers double coupons. You can also get twice as much by watching for "buy one/get one free" offers.

- **Price Competitors' Ads**

    If you shop at stores (such as Super Wal-Mart) that offer to match the price of their competitors, you can take in all the sale ads for the week to one central location and they will match them. You'll save gas, time, and money.

Kids' Rooms

- *Delayed gratification.* When your child wants the latest toy advertised in a commercial, you don't have to run out and buy it. If the neighbors buy their child a new bike, you don't have to buy one for Junior. When you're in the store and your little precious sees some cool candy, you don't have to instantly fulfill his every whim! Delayed gratification saves money and teaches our children to develop internal controls, a characteristic that will help them as adults.

- *Saving for a rainy day.* Three of my children were

saving money for new bikes in the spring. (They'll be less likely to leave these valued bikes out in the rain when they've earned a portion of their purchase.) The other day, when they were helping me cut coupons, they found a coupon for bikes ordered through Huffy. They paid a third less than a discount store, and the purchase price included delivery.

- *They pay for upgrades.* When your teen has to have the latest tennis shoes to the tune of $150, just say, "I'll pay $45 for tennis shoes. Anything more than that you can earn." This teaches teens the value of a dollar. If they hold out their no-longer-pudgy hands and say they want to go to Six Flags, let them earn the price of the ticket and give them some spending money if you wish.

- *Entertainment alternatives.* The local library offers a lot of inexpensive fun for children. They can borrow videos, books-on-tape, CDs, and audiocassettes, besides the ever-popular books. Many libraries have a story time and special summer camps for kids.

- *It's not crazy-mas, it's Christ-mas!* We told the Kay family babes years ago that if three gifts was good enough for baby Jesus, three gifts is good enough for them. This tradition has kept the focus of the season where it belongs, and it's kept us out of debt, too.

- *Young entrepreneurs.* Earning money helps build self-esteem and encourages responsibility. Keep in mind, though, that children need supervision and accountability in their work endeavors. Teach your children to finish the job, do it well, and do it in a timely manner. In the Kay household we require that our kids stick with something for at least a year before they're allowed to quit—whether it's violin lessons or a newspaper route. Remember to teach your child to "tithe" part of their job. If they walk dogs, encourage them to walk the dog of an elderly neighbor on a fixed income for free. If they baby-sit, suggest they offer a free night out for a single mom in the church. They may discover that the most gratifying work is the kind where they do it out of God's love for their neighbor.

For a free download of "Cash for Kids," which provides kids and parents details about specific jobs, go to www.elliekay.com.

The Master Bedroom

Second Honeymoon Getaways

When it comes to saving money, it's important to save while still preserving the most important relationship—the one between you and your spouse. To make your savings even more valuable, you might want to put some of the money you "save" each week into a special "second honeymoon" account (the "Fun Money" savings) so the two of you can get away for a "Seventh-Day Rest." I know of several couples who did this and were able to splurge on their anniversary with a special trip. This is not only good financial stewardship, but it's a fabulous investment in your marriage. Here are a few tips to make sure that you don't let the budget for your second honeymoon getaway get away from you:

- **Set Priorities** Establish some goals for your trip and what you can live with (and what you can't live without). If you want an exotic location, you may have to settle for fewer days away from home. For example, you might choose a four-day vacation to Hawaii as your only trip in three years over a week at a nearby resort each year.
- **Use a Travel Agent** To get an idea of what your dream honeymoon will cost, go to an agent. They get specials on air/hotel packages due to their high business volume. If you're still not convinced you're getting the best deal, then go to some of the following travel sites to compare prices.
- **Internet Savings** For the best rates on hotels, airfares, and car rentals check out the prices at such sites as *www.travelocity.com, www.cheaptickets.com, www.expedia.com, www.webflyer.com,* and *www.orbitz.com. After* you get a price and *before* you book a fare, go directly to that airline's Web site to check out their cheapest fares. Some good hotel brokers that buy up a block of rooms and pass along the savings are: *www.quickbook.com* and *www.1800usahotels.com.* Be sure to read the fine print of any offer so you understand the restrictions and limitations associated with a cheaper fare.
- **Travel Off-Season** By traveling during an off-peak time you'll not only save money, you won't fight the crowds, either. According to Consumer Reports Travel Letter, the optimum time to get the best airline fares is October through early December and January through March. The fares are even better if you stay over a Saturday night.

- **A Strong Dollar Close to Home** If you live near Canada or Mexico, your dollar could go a lot further because of the weak local currencies in these areas. If you use a credit card for the majority of your purchases, you will not pay a fee for converting your dollars into the foreign currency.

Home Office

- **Online Codes** Before you order anything off the Internet, whether it's electronic equipment, clothing, a book, or a CD, check the savings codes. Often online e-tailers will offer special discounts if you know the code to enter. Before you order online, go to one of the code sources to see if there's a discount listed for the e-tailer and/or the product you want. These discounts could be percentages off, free postage, or even free gifts with your purchase. Go to *www.currentcodes.com, www.coolsavings.com* (also linked to my website), *www.dealcatcher.com,* or *www.edealfinder.com.*
- **Cell Phones** Visit *www.MyRatePlan.com;* the site will ask you questions about your total minutes, weekend vs. weekdays, and whether you need free long distance or free roaming, then it points you to the best plan for you. It's the most comprehensive site of its type.
- **Long Distance** Usually the cheapest long distance is found on the 3.5 cent/minute calling cards available at Sam's Club and Costco. But if that is too inconvenient for your time investment, then go to *www.LowerMyBills.com* to see what the best rate is for you and your needs.
- **Online Banking** *www.Gomez.com* has a survey of

online banks that is updated twice a year. You can tell the search engine which aspect of banking—i.e., cost, ease of use—is most important to you, or whether you're a saver or a borrower, and it will customize its recommendation.

In conclusion, just remember that *you don't have to do all of these!* You don't even have to do the majority of them. But if you will apply a few of these each week, you will find that the satisfaction of getting a financial return for a little bit of effort can be quite satisfying. You might even find that you are getting addicted to saving money, in which case you'll need to review the chapter on "The Seventh-Day Rest" again!

twelve

The Giving Tree
Smart Ways to Be Generous

One afternoon on the way to the grocery store, my then five-year-old son, Joshua, and his four-year-old friend, Rachel, were playing with their toys in the backseat of the van.

Rachel tossed her blond curls and looked at Joshua with big blue eyes. She smiled sweetly. "My daddy brought me back these Minnie Mouse dolls when he went to the state of Cal-do-forn-ya."

Rough-and-tumble Joshua replied, "Oh yeah? Well, my papa got me these Star War toys for my birthday, and look what I can do with them!"

There were a series of gutteral noises followed by feminine distress signals during which Minnie fell victim to a light saber.

"Oh no! Joshua!" Rachel grabbed her doll. "She doesn't wike to be poked; let's have a tea party instead."

By the time we got to the store, a doe-eyed doll had tamed the Jedi knight. Once inside, we decided to purchase fried chicken from the grocery deli for lunch. Joshua wanted a whole chicken, and Rachel wanted only one leg. After some cajoling, we compromised on a five-piece box of chicken for $2.99. We sat in a booth, and the kids ate happily while I watched them. I wasn't really hungry and planned on having the two untouched pieces of chicken later that afternoon. I had the box with the price on it and was planning on paying for it with the rest of my groceries at the checkout.

Suddenly a man, who looked like a homeless person, walked into the eating area, interrupting our reverie. His worn face showed years of tough living as he muttered to himself, his head twitching in small, sharp movements. He sat down across the aisle from us and turned in his chair to stare at the three ladies eating at the table next to him. The women quickly decided they were finished with lunch, cleared off their table, and left. Everyone else in the deli area politely ignored him. As we were getting ready to leave, I thought, *You know, I donate lots of food with my couponing to the local homeless shelter to feed guys like him.* I comforted my conscience with the idea that I was indirectly doing something for the man.

Just then Rachel spilled her water on the floor. I grabbed a handful of napkins, and crouching over the mess on the floor, I was only inches away from the man's battered boots. I could see the worn soles and weather-beaten leather revealed several holes. It was while I was in this humble position that another thought came into my mind: *Give him the rest of the chicken in the box.* In one hand I held a wad of wet napkins to be discarded, and with the other hand I picked up the box, held it out to the man, and softly asked, "Would you like some chicken?"

His dark-skinned face suddenly brightened, revealing a toothless grin as he responded enthusiastically, "Yes! Thank you very much!" He held out his hands, displaying several fingers that had been amputated. The entire exchange took less than ten seconds as I smiled and whispered, "You're welcome." But the mental image of this poor man reaching out to me to receive the food has remained etched in my mind.

As I turned away to throw away the sopping mess of napkins, I felt a tug at my side followed by a little boy's voice, "Gee, Mama, that was a nice thing to do!" Then off he ran with Rachel to get their free cookies at the bakery counter.

As soon as I rounded the corner to follow them, a dark thought crossed my mind. *You know, you haven't paid for the chicken yet. You were going to pay for it with your groceries. When you go through the checkout, no one will know, and you don't have the box with the price on it anymore. You could give that man the chicken for free.*

Isn't it amazing how the enemy of good is right there, waiting to rob us of a blessing through his empty promises and skewed rationalization? My counter-thought was *To steal a blessing is no blessing at all. My integrity is worth more than $2.99.*

Cookies in hand, I gathered my ruddy son and his delicate girl friend and headed toward the checkout. After paying for the groceries and the deli purchase, I loaded the kids into the car. As we drove away, a still, small voice spoke to my heart: *When you've done it to the least of these, Ellie, you've done it unto me.*

———

One man, one small box of chicken, one busy mom, and one observant son. All were impacted in one spontaneous opportunity to obey a prompting from within. Would this act of giving make a difference in the old man's life? Would the son recall his mother's generosity? Would the blessing be robbed so quickly after it was bestowed? Would Minnie Mouse recover from her light saber wounds? Only time can answer these questions in my life and in yours. But one thing is certain: There is power in a gift.

———

My original book, *Shop, Save, and Share,* surprised everyone: my agent, my publishing house, and myself! I was an unknown first-time female author without a huge ministry or a large following—and the book became a bestseller. My editor told me that at one point the publishing team was sitting in a meeting discussing sales numbers on various projects, when my book came up. All the experienced professionals tried to reason why this book sold so many more copies than expected. One of the guys remarked, "Must be God."

Cool.

The one item that sets my approach to finances apart is the idea of saving for a reason beyond just your own family's well- being. I've always encouraged people to save in order to share—and it works.

I can't tell you how gratifying it is to get letters and e-mails from people who have been blessed by the concept of "extravagant giving" and have given away food, clothes, and even cars. Each and every person has a positive experience from giving in this way. I've yet to receive an e-mail that says, *"Hey, Ellie! I gave some food to a homeless man and he had a meal that day because of the food I gave him. Well, that made me feel really lousy. I wish I hadn't shared with him."*

Nope. I don't get those kinds of e-mails.

Instead, I get e-mails telling me that when they gave, they never really knew how good it could feel. Generosity begets generosity. When one homeless shelter had a Suburban donated to them so that they could "ride the rails" of the train tracks and pick up homeless men, the story was published in the paper. The shelter then received a donation of a remodeled shower and bathroom to accommodate these people, and they also received cash donations and contributions of all kinds!

It's also important that you teach your children to be generous, because it is quite likely that it will not come naturally to your child to give of his time and energy. A lot of the ideas in this chapter also detail ways that your children can help in their communities. Who knows where your generosity will lead through the ripple effect? But you have to make that first splash before you can look for any kind of contagious effect.

The Giving Tree

In the bestselling children's book *The Giving Tree,* the story begins, "Once there was a tree . . . and she loved a little boy" (HarperCollins, 2002). This is a story of unforgettable perception, beautifully written and illustrated by Shel Silverstein.

Every day the boy would come to the tree to eat her apples, swing from her branches, or slide down her trunk . . . and the tree was happy. But as the boy grew older he began to want more from the tree, and the tree gave and gave and gave.

This is a tender story, touched with sadness, aglow with consolation. The interpretation of the gift of giving and an acceptance of another's capacity to love in return are two central themes to this book. But it seems that the author leaves some of the meanings of the book open to interpretation because it ends with nothing left of the tree but a stump. You could either infer that the tree gave too much or that the boy, who became an old man, took too much. Or, you could deduce that the tree was happy in giving until it could give no more.

Do You Give Too Much or Too Little?

Overall, Americans are tremendously generous. The statistics indicate that people with modest means out-give those with the greatest means. On the average, Americans, at almost all income levels, give around 3 percent of their income to charity—which is a lot for those who are living from paycheck to paycheck but quite little for those who are wealthy. Andrew Tobias, a financial writer for *Parade Magazine,* said, "One very decent millionaire I know felt too stressed to grant an important $10,000 request because, he said, he had just spent $80,000 on wall coverings" (November 2001).

Contrast that with Oseola McCarty, a Mississippi laundress of very humble means, who never owned a car and had to walk a mile to the grocery store. At the age of eighty-seven, she astonished everyone by giving $150,000, which was her entire life savings, to establish a college scholarship. As God blesses you to be able to give, you will need discernment in choosing the organization to which you will donate. Here are some ideas to consider.

Getting Started

So what if you've never been a big giver before? I hear from scores of people who were not raised with a giving mindset and are excited about the prospect of giving away food, time, talent, and money. The best place to get started is locally. Here are some places in your own neighborhood:

- **The Local Church** Bob and I, even when we were as poor as church mice, gave 10 percent of our income to our local church. The church, in turn, taught our family spiritual values, ran kids' programs in the summers, provided food and clothing to orphanages in Mexico, and sent money to missionaries overseas—to name a few things. But what if you're not sure you "trust" your local church to be a good steward of your money? What if your pastor drives a Ferrari and has a diamond bigger than Zsa Zsa Gabor's engagement ring from her tenth husband? The good news is you can choose where you go to church and to which church you will give your tithe! So you see, there aren't really any excuses for not supporting your local church community.

- **Homeless Shelters** Those who volunteer at these shelters and donate food, clothing, finances, or their time are truly on the front lines. There's nothing like a day of serving food at one of these shelters or soup kitchens to make a family thankful for things they might otherwise take for granted. Our family tries to help people when we see them "flying a sign" (as I've been told it's called) that reads, "Will Work for Food." Homeless director Kris King says, "Never give these people money because they will likely spend it on alcohol. Instead, give them the name and address of the local homeless shelter or give them canned food." Kris also said, "Some of these people are not homeless at all; they make upwards of $50 an hour by panhandling professionally and then return to their homes at night."

At the age of nine, Daniel came up with the idea of keeping canned goods in our Suburban. We would hand each person two cans of chili or pasta meals. When we first started doing this, the kids were so enthusiastic to help that they saw a homeless person behind every bush. One day we were driving down the road when then seven-year-old Philip yelled, "Hey! There's a homeless man!"

To which I replied, "Philip! That man is not homeless; he doesn't have a sign, he's on a bicycle, and his jeans are just dirty."

Philip sighed, "Well, he looked kind of lost to me. Maybe we could give him some clothes soap!"

It's the thought that counts.

- **Crisis Pregnancy Centers** These centers provide assistance to women in crisis pregnancies by giving tangible help in the form of medical care, clothes, toiletries, baby food, groceries, and sometimes housing. Check your local phone book to find one near you.
- **Orphanages and Children's Homes** There may not be a local orphanage, but your church or civic organization may have regular access to these institutions. Contact these organizations and see what kind of "needs list" they may have. Often these lists are very specific due to the age, gender, and size of their children as well as their nutritional requirements. Living in New Mexico gave us a great opportunity to visit Mexican orphanages in Juarez, Mexico, as well as Native American tribal reservation outreaches.
- **Women's Shelters** Women and children who seek these shelters often arrive with only the clothes on

their backs. These shelters especially need trial-size toiletries, as their occupants may stay for a day or for several months, as well as children's and women's clothing. Look in the Yellow Pages under "Spouse Abuse" for the phone number. Don't be surprised if you are asked to drop off these donations at a downtown office rather than the home itself—confidentiality is necessary for the protection of these clients.

Over a six-month period, I got thirty-five bottles of hair coloring free with my couponing. These were donated to this shelter with the understanding that the women could exchange them in the local grocery store for the right shade. Sometimes it's the little things that make the difference in a difficult situation.

- **Postal Workers Food Drive** Every year postal workers collect millions of pounds of nonperishable food for people in need. In addition, there are Boy Scout/ Girl Scout food drives and others throughout the community. Your child's school or your church may also have occasional food drives to stock community food pantries. A *Shop, Save, and Share* graduate, Brenda Conway, said, "I used to donate two cans of food to my son's Boy Scout food drive—now I'm able to donate two bags of groceries, and I don't spend any more than I did before."
- **Salvation Army and Goodwill** These nonprofit groups help support disabled Americans through the provision of jobs. Be sure to drop off your donations during business hours so you can secure a tax-deductible receipt. They also help provide clothing to developing-nation organizations. The amount of clothing they've sent overseas in the last twenty years

could fill 30,000 Sam's Club stores! That's a good amount of cotton.

Reaching Beyond Our Borders

Even before I published *Shop, Save, and Share,* I determined that a portion of the proceeds would go to a mission organization called Mission of Joy. A friend of ours, Colonel Jeff O'Leary, founded it over a decade ago. When he was a captain in the Air Force, he traveled to India and was forever impacted by the extreme need among children in that country. Through his organization, our family has sponsored a variety of children over the last decade. We've even had the privilege of seeing some of them grow up, marry, and continue the work to their own native people.

Mission of Joy is a nonprofit organization whose purpose is to reach India with the gospel and provide food, clothing, shelter, and education to otherwise destitute and homeless children. Mission of Joy (MOJ) has built numerous churches and three orphanages in Andhra Pradesh, South India. Mission of Joy is not funded or supported by one church or denomination.

Even now, my product manager sends out a brochure on MOJ with every book we ship, and there are scores of children who are now sponsored because of the commitment by the *Shop, Save, and Share* ministry. You can view their Web site at *www.missionjoy.org* or write to them at:

Mission of Joy
P.O. Box 64914
Tacoma, WA 98464

The e-mail contact for information about Mission

of Joy, child sponsorship, or native missionary sponsorship is Jeff O'Leary at *jeffreyoleary@jeffoleary.com.*

Tax-Smart Giving

Double Up

We've already mentioned that you should get a tax-deductible receipt for your giving, but what if you're just getting started and don't think you'll have enough deductions to itemize on your income tax return? You could "double up" on your giving by deferring your normal year-end gifts from December to January. Then give your regular gifts that December of the same year. This "doubling up" will likely give you the amount you need to itemize.

Don't Fund Overhead or Fund-Raising

You don't want your dollars going to pay fat salaries, fancy overhead, or excessive fund-raising expenses. The Better Business Bureau's (BBB) Wise Giving Alliance offers guidance to donors on making informed giving decisions through their charity evaluations, various "tips" publications, and the quarterly "Better Business Bureau Wise Giving Guide." You can access this information by calling (703) 276-0100, going to *www.give.org,* or writing them for free publications at:

BBB Wise Giving Alliance
4200 Wilson Blvd, Suite 800
Arlington, VA 22203

You can ask them to mail you the various tip guides

or read them online. These guides include information on:

Charitable giving
Police and fire fighter organizations
Handling unwanted direct mail from charitable organizations
Child sponsorship organizations
Direct mail sweepstakes and charities
Contributing used cars to charities
Tax deductions for charitable contributions

Save Receipts

You should save all receipts for donations of $250 or more if you itemize. So if you give away more than $250 worth of clothing throughout the year, you should have saved all the receipts that will add up to that amount. You must donate these to a nonprofit organization or have that organization donate it to another needy individual. The money you donate directly to a needy person is not deductible. It would be better to donate the amount to your church and have it anonymously send the donation to the family in need. Check with your tax specialist every year for the latest tax laws.

Starting Your Own Foundation

If you are blessed enough to be sitting on a large gain from a stock or mutual fund that you have held for over a year, consider using it to become what is essentially your own "foundation." For example, if you own $10,000 worth of stock that you bought years ago for only $3,000, you can donate the stock by setting up a Fidelity Charitable Gift Fund account (call 1-800-682-

4438 or go to *www.charitablegift.org*). By doing this, you get an immediate $10,000 tax deduction and save having to pay taxes on the $7,000 gain. In the years to come, as that $10,000 grows, you get to instruct the company that manages your "foundation" where to donate the proceeds. Besides Fidelity, there are also charitable gift funds available through Vanguard at 1-888-383-4483 or *www.vanguardcharitable.org*, or Schwab at 1-800-746-6216 or *www.schwabcharitable.org*. It is a convenient, tax-savvy way to give.

Kid Philanthropists

Around November, let your children know that you will allow them to manage a donation in a predetermined amount ($25, $50, or whatever you have budgeted). They get to research a variety of nonprofit organizations and decide which one will receive their donation. Then donate the amount in your child's name. You get the tax benefit, your child gets the thank-you note, and you both feel good about giving.

Twenty Free Gifts You Can Give

I'd like to end this book with gifts that are of tremendous, even eternal, value at no cost to you.

1. *Fix broken fences by mending a quarrel.*
2. *Seek out a friend you haven't seen in a while or who has been forgotten.*
3. *Hug someone and whisper, "I love you."*
4. *Forgive an enemy and pray for him or her.*
5. *Be patient with an angry person.*
6. *Express gratitude to someone in your world.*
7. *Make a child smile.*

8. *Find the time to keep a promise.*
9. *Make or bake something for someone else—anonymously.*
10. *Speak kindly to a stranger and tell them a joke.*
11. *Enter into another's sorrows and cut the pain in half.*
12. *Smile. Laugh a little. Laugh a lot.*
13. *Take a walk with a friend.*
14. *Kneel down and pat a dog.*
15. *Lessen your expectations of others.*
16. *Apologize if you were wrong.*
17. *Turn off the television and talk.*
18. *Pray for someone who helped you when you hurt.*
19. *Give a soft answer even though you feel strongly.*
20. *Encourage an older person.*

(Paraphrased from Chuck Swindoll, *The Finishing Touch* [Word Publishing, 1994].)

Who knows, this might be the most valuable portion of this book. I'd like you to indulge me for a minute as I ask you to go back and reread that list. As you read these through a second time, write down the ones that seem to speak to you personally. You might even put them on a Post-it note where you can be reminded to try one a day, a week, or a month. If you do so, within a month you will make giving gifts a daily habit.

————

This week our local radio station had a contest in which entrants wrote to tell why they deserved to win a "Super Bowl Party Package," which included a brand-new nineteen-inch television and a satellite dish. I wrote the following story:

The Super Bowl Fairy Tale

Once upon a time, there was a raven-haired maiden with alabaster skin and a furrowed brow. Her hair was black because she was young and had not yet earned the right to gray hairs. Her skin was like alabaster because she used Mary Kay products from her youth. Alas, her brow was furrowed because she was unhappy. She only had self-centered, tobacco-chewin', red-necked beaus in her fair country of Texasania.

How she longed for a fair prince to visit her country, fly her away from all the Bubbas, and bestow her with her heart's desire—the moon. One evening she stood outside gazing at the star-studded heavens, breathing in the blossom-scented air, and praying God would send her heart's desire. At that precise moment, the maiden saw a falling star. This was no ordinary falling star, for it had a crimson glow attached to its ethereal light. She made a wish. All of a sudden, she realized the star was an airplane. Since the maid was also an astrodynamics major (in her spare time), she knew it was no ordinary airplane—it was a stealth F–117, the most celebrated, manly airplane in the global kingdom!

The aviator was a virtual Adonis—with a bushy "guard" mustache and lots of hair on his cranium. Her heart beat madly. The handsome prince spied the fair maiden, and he promptly swept her off her feet, promising to fly her away from Bubbaville and give her the moon. They were wed in a fairy-tale setting and settled into the happily-ever-afters of life.

Prince Charming became known as "Papa" to five babies in seven years. He showed his bride the world with eight moves in ten years. Day after day he slipped the surly bonds of earth and danced the sky on laughter's silver wings. Meanwhile, the maiden's raven hair earned the distinctive privilege of silver threads. Her alabaster skin began to furrow at the brow as she sipped potty water (accidentally, that's another story).

The king was assigned to the kingdom of Alamogordo and served his country in exotic locations such as Hawaii, Boston, and Las Vegas.

Meanwhile, the queen had "help" with her daily chores. In grocery shopping, the youngest two royal heirs, Jonathan and Joshua, assisted her by throwing Attends bladder control products into her cart. When the checker refused to void these purchases off her bill, she carried the royalty thing a bit too far. She had the poor cashier clapped in irons and thrown into the dungeon. The clerks learned that one does not mess with folks from Texasania.

The royal family did not see their wealth as something to be used exclusively for themselves. While in the kingdom of Alamogordo, they provided for the underprivileged, those who were forgotten, and those who had no homes. The royal children gathered bags of groceries to take to the homeless shelter. They collected towels to donate to the day shelter, where these people could get a shower and a shave. This middle class royal family even donated their royal carriage—a Suburban—to this shelter so that the director could "ride the rails" and pick up the homeless at their camps by the railroad tracks. In the vehicle formerly occupied by the royal children, homeless men are driving to rehab centers to start a new life. They're transported to the social security office in Las Cruces—a first step toward becoming gainfully employed.

This family learned that wealth, riches, and honor are of no value unless they are shared in community with those who need to learn how to help themselves. Recently, the royals heard of a "Super Bowl" contest sponsored by 94KEY—

the winners would get a new television, a satellite system, and food. They decided, as a family, to enter the contest with the express purpose of donating the television and satellite system to the homeless shelter so that those who would have no hope of watching the Super Bowl could have that privilege.

And the royals, in giving to others, learned the secret of living happily ever after.

The things that matter most in life are the things you give away.

I got the call yesterday.

I won.

Truly.

I was so excited to call the homeless shelter director and tell her of the new television and satellite dish she would receive. She was ecstatic! Tomorrow they will deliver the package to the Kays, which also includes a year's worth of pizzas, a six-foot submarine sandwich, and a huge supply of Pepsi. I wish you could join in on our party tomorrow.

In fact, you *can* join in on the "party" of living well and giving well. I have enjoyed our time together, and if this book has left you with anything, I hope it leaves you with the idea that the things that matter most in life are the things you give away.

ELLIE KAY is a bestselling, award-winning author, national radio commentator, and regular media guest as well as a gifted speaker. She is a graduate of Colorado Christian University with a degree in the management of human resources. She and her husband, Bob, a contract fighter pilot with a major aerospace corporation, have five children at home and two adult children and make their home in Southern California.

If you wish to contact Ellie Kay for speaking engagements, media, or seminars, she can be reached at:

Ellie Kay
% Speak Up Speaker Services
1614 Edison Shores Place
Port Huron, MI 48060
speakupinc@aol.com

e-mail: ellie@elliekay.com
Web site: *www.elliekay.com*

Financial Expert®

Simplify, Spend Less, & *Give* More!